TIME-LIFE FAVORITE RECIPES

CHICKEN

Alexandria, Virginia

Time-Life Books is a division of Time Life Inc.

TIME LIFE INC.
President and CEO: George Artandi

TIME-LIFE CUSTOM PUBLISHING
Vice President and Publisher: Terry Newell
Vice President of Sales and Marketing: Neil Levin
Director of Special Sales: Liz Ziehl
Editor for Special Markets: Anna Burgard
Production Manager: Carolyn Bounds
Quality Assurance Manager: James D. King
Pre-press Services: Time-Life Imaging Center

SPECIAL CONTRIBUTORS
Editing: Betty Bianconi, In Good Taste
Design: Anna Burgard
Design Production: Ruth Thompson, Thunder Hill Graphics
Proofreading: Celia Beattie
Index: Judy Davis

This book is an adaptation of the Time Life series *Creative Everyday Cooking* © 1990

10 9 8 7 6 5 4 3 2
Printed in China

ISBN: 0-7370-1113-0

CIP data available upon application:
Librarian, Time-Life Books
2000 Duke Street
Alexandria, Virginia 22314

TABLE OF CONTENTS

INTRODUCTION

CHANCES ARE, your family will be eating chicken sometime this week. You may have some in the refrigerator or on your shopping list right now. And why not? Chicken is healthy, economical, and easy to prepare. Chicken's subtle flavor lends itself to almost any seasoning or style of cooking, and it can be prepared quickly. A boneless chicken breast can sauté on top of the stove in as little as 10 minutes. A whole chicken can be roasted in under an hour. Chicken is one of the most versatile foods available—you can bake, broil, stir-fry, or grill it; prepare it in soups and salads; marinate or bread it. It can be spiced, diced, sliced, shredded, or barbecued. No wonder Americans eat billions of pounds of chicken every year!

You probably have some favorite chicken recipes that you return to time and again because they're quick, delicious—and easy. Now, the editors of Time-Life Books will help you discover 100 new, exciting ways to prepare chicken without having to spend lots of time, buy exotic ingredients or learn complicated preparation techniques that take you out of your daily routine. These simple, easy-to-follow recipes range from basic, homey dishes like Crispy Oven-Fried Chicken and Chicken Pot Pie to classic international favorites like Chicken Cordon Bleu and Chicken Marsala.

Here are tempting recipes that can be prepared with basic ingredients available in your grocery store—no long lists of unrecognized ingredients to buy from the gourmet store! The editors of Time-Life Books show you how to prepare delicious meals with a few quick and simple steps. Most dishes can be prepared in under thirty minutes, so even after a busy day you can sit down to a tasty and nutritious meal without a lot of fuss. Each recipe is accompanied by nutritional information, such as fat, sodium, and protein content, so you know what you're feeding your family. There are handy preparation and serving tips, and of course, beautiful full-color photos of many of the dishes. And the book lies flat, so you won't have to keep rummaging to find your place.

Time-Life Favorite Recipes: Chicken takes you from hearty soups and stews, easy and elegant appetizers, and savory salads through a variety of main course dishes. Learn to prepare ethnic or regional classics like Chicken Soup with Matzo Balls, Chicken Jambalaya, or Oriental Chicken and Rice Salad. Serve cool Minted Chicken Salad or Chicken Cobb Salad in the heat of summer; prepare a robust Chicken Stroganoff or Brunswick Stew on cold winter nights. Hungry for a dish with lots of vegetables? Try Chicken Vegetable Stir Fry. Excite your taste buds with Pepper-Pecan Chicken or Szechwan Chicken Wings. For a change of pace, serve up Lime-Grilled Chicken Sandwiches or Stovetop Barbecued Burgers.

You'll find that after using this book you'll have a whole new roster of quick and easy chicken favorites to fall back on! So go ahead and treat yourself and your family to a whole new way of enjoying one of your favorite foods—chicken!

Chicken and Tiny Star Pasta Stew

Miniature star pasta is sometimes called "stelline" or "pastina," although rice-shaped pasta or even alphabets can be used.

Serves 4

2 TABLESPOONS BUTTER OR MARGARINE
3 TABLESPOONS ALL-PURPOSE FLOUR
3 CUPS CHICKEN BROTH
¾ TEASPOON DRIED THYME
¼ TEASPOON PEPPER
½ CUP TINY PASTA STARS OR OTHER SMALL PASTA SHAPES
2 LARGE CARROTS, THINLY SLICED
¼ POUND MUSHROOMS, THINLY SLICED
1 POUND SKINLESS, BONELESS CHICKEN BREASTS, CUT INTO BITE-SIZE PIECES
10 CHERRY TOMATOES
1 SMALL BUNCH GREEN ONIONS (ABOUT 6), CHOPPED

1 In large saucepan, melt the butter over medium heat. Stir in the flour and cook, stirring, until the flour has completely absorbed the butter, about 1 minute.

2 Increase heat to medium-high; slowly add a small amount of chicken broth; stir until well combined. Gradually add remaining chicken broth, thyme and pepper; bring to a boil, stirring occasionally, until slightly thickened.

3 Add the pasta and carrots and cook, uncovered, about 3 minutes.

4 Add the mushrooms, chicken and whole tomatoes. Return the mixture to a boil over medium-high heat, breaking up the tomatoes with a spoon.

5 Reduce the heat to medium-low; cover and simmer until the chicken is cooked through, about 5 minutes. Stir in green onions.

PREPARATION TIP
This stew can be made in advance and reheated gently on the stovetop or in the microwave.

Calories: 320 · Protein: 32 g
Fat: 8 g/22% calories from fat · Carbohydrate: 28 g
Cholesterol: 81 mg · Sodium: 649 mg

Chunky Chicken-Potato Soup

Serves 4

- **4** TABLESPOONS BUTTER OR MARGARINE
- **¼** CUP ALL-PURPOSE FLOUR
- **4½** CUPS CHICKEN BROTH
- **2** MEDIUM ALL-PURPOSE POTATOES, PEELED AND CUT INTO ½-INCH CUBES
- **1** MEDIUM ONION, COARSELY CHOPPED
- **¼** TEASPOON PEPPER
- **1½** CUPS CUBED COOKED CHICKEN (ABOUT 8 OUNCES)
- **1½** CUPS MILK
- **1** CAN (16 OUNCES) WHOLE-KERNEL CORN, DRAINED
- **1** CUP BROCCOLI FLORETS

1 In a large saucepan, melt the butter over medium heat until hot but not smoking, about 2 to 3 minutes.

2 Stir in flour; cook, stirring constantly, until the flour and butter are completely blended, about 1 minute.

3 Slowly pour in the chicken broth, stirring constantly. Return mixture to a boil. Add potatoes, onion and pepper; reduce the heat to medium-low. Cover and simmer, stirring occasionally, until potatoes are tender, about 15 minutes.

4 Increase the heat to medium and return to a boil. Stir in the chicken, milk, corn and broccoli. Cook until the broccoli is crisp-tender and the chicken is heated through, 2 to 3 minutes.

Calories: 471 · Protein: 28 g
Fat: 22 g/42% calories from fat · Carbohydrate: 44 g
Cholesterol: 94 mg · Sodium: 1,354 mg

Chicken and Rice in Green Vegetable Broth

Serves 4

- **3** CUPS CHICKEN BROTH
- **2** CUPS WATER
- **½** CUP LONG-GRAIN RICE
- **1** TEASPOON DRIED THYME
- **½** TEASPOON PEPPER
- **2** CHICKEN LEGS (ABOUT 14 OUNCES), SKINNED
- **2** CUPS SHREDDED CABBAGE (ABOUT 6 OUNCES)
- **2** CUPS FRESH SPINACH LEAVES, SHREDDED

1 In a large saucepan, combine the chicken broth, water, rice, thyme and pepper. Add chicken; cover and bring to a boil over high heat. Reduce the heat to low and simmer, about 15 minutes.

2 Transfer the chicken to a cutting board. Remove meat from the bones and cut it into bite-size pieces.

3 Return the chicken pieces to the broth mixture. Add the cabbage and spinach and bring to a boil over medium-high heat. Boil just until the cabbage and spinach are wilted and the chicken is heated through, about 1 minute.

PREPARATION TIP
To save time washing, trimming and shredding fresh spinach, thaw and use half of a 10-ounce package of frozen chopped spinach.

Calories: 191 · Protein: 16 g
Fat: 4 g/18% calories from fat · Carbohydrate: 23 g
Cholesterol: 45 mg · Sodium: 119 mg

Ham, White Bean and Sweet Potato Soup

Serves 6

2½ CUPS CHICKEN BROTH
1 CUP WATER
2 CLOVES GARLIC, MINCED
1 TEASPOON DIJON MUSTARD
¼ TEASPOON PEPPER
1 BAY LEAF
1 CAN (16 OUNCES) SMALL WHITE BEANS, RINSED AND DRAINED
1 MEDIUM SWEET POTATO (ABOUT 8 OUNCES), CUT INTO ½-INCH PIECES
1 CUP DICED COOKED CHICKEN (ABOUT 8 OUNCES)
2 GREEN ONIONS, COARSELY CHOPPED

1 In large saucepan or Dutch oven, combine chicken broth, water, garlic, mustard, pepper and bay leaf; cover and bring to a boil over medium-high heat.

2 Add beans and sweet potato. Reduce the heat to medium-low; cover and simmer until sweet potato is cooked through, about 20 to 25 minutes.

3 Add chicken and green onions; cook until heated through, about 2 to 3 minutes. Discard bay leaf.

PREPARATION TIP
This is a great dish for using leftover chicken or turkey. If none is on hand, buy a thick slice of chicken roll from the deli counter and dice. For variations, try using cooked chicken sausage, cut into pieces, or tiny meatballs made from ground chicken.

Calories: 218 · Protein: 20 g
Fat: 4 g/16% calories from fat · Carbohydrate: 25 g
Cholesterol: 34 mg · Sodium: 371 mg

Chicken Soup with Matzo Balls

Serves 4

1 BROILER-FRYER (3 TO 3½ POUNDS) WITH NECK AND GIBLETS
8 CUPS WATER
2 ONIONS, QUARTERED
2 RIBS CELERY WITH LEAVES, CUT INTO 4 PIECES
2 CARROTS, CUT INTO 4 PIECES
2 CLOVES GARLIC, PEELED
4 TO 6 SPRIGS PARSLEY
2 SPRIGS FRESH OR ½ TEASPOON DRIED THYME
1 TEASPOON WHOLE BLACK PEPPERCORNS
1 BAY LEAF
2 TEASPOONS SALT
PREPARED MATZO BALLS (RECIPE BELOW)

1 In large saucepan or Dutch oven, place broiler-fryer, water, onions, celery, carrots, garlic, parsley, thyme, peppercorns, bay leaf and salt over high heat. Bring to a boil; reduce heat to low, cover and simmer until chicken is tender, about 45 to 60 minutes.

2 Remove chicken; skin and remove the meat from the bones. Cut the meat into bite-size pieces; set aside. Discard the skin, bones, giblets and neck. Strain the broth and discard the vegetables and herbs. If necessary, skim off fat.

3 Return broth to saucepan. Bring to a simmer over low heat; add the matzo balls. Cook, uncovered, until matzo balls rise to the top and are fluffy, about 30 to 40 minutes. Stir in reserved chicken meat.

Matzo Balls: In medium bowl, beat together 4 eggs, 1 cup matzo meal, ⅓ cup chicken broth or water, 3 tablespoons chicken fat or oil, 1 teaspoon salt and ½ teaspoon white pepper until thoroughly blended. With hands, shape mixture into 2-inch balls. Cook as directed above.

Calories: 534 · Protein: 47 g
Fat: 26 g/46% calories from fat · Carbohydrate: 23 g
Cholesterol: 369 mg · Sodium: 1,846 mg

Chicken Corn Chowder

Serves 4

- **1** TABLESPOON OLIVE OIL
- **1** LARGE ONION, FINELY CHOPPED
- **1** RED PEPPER, DICED
- **1** ALL-PURPOSE POTATO, PEELED AND DICED
- **1** OUNCE CANADIAN BACON, DICED
- **1** CUP CHICKEN BROTH
- **1** CUP EVAPORATED SKIM MILK
- **1** CAN (8¾ OUNCES) CREAMED CORN
- **¾** POUND SKINLESS, BONELESS CHICKEN BREASTS, DICED
- **¾** CUP FROZEN OR CANNED, DRAINED, WHOLE-KERNEL CORN
- **½** TEASPOON SALT
- **¼** TEASPOON PEPPER
- CHOPPED PARSLEY (OPTIONAL)

1 In a medium saucepan, heat oil over medium heat. Add the onion, red pepper, potato and bacon. Cook, covered, until vegetables begin to soften, about 5 minutes, stirring occasionally.

2 Stir in the broth, milk and creamed corn. Bring to a boil. Reduce the heat to low and simmer, uncovered, about 10 minutes, stirring occasionally.

3 Stir in the chicken, whole-kernel corn, salt and pepper. Cook until the chicken is cooked through, about 7 to 10 minutes. Serve sprinkled with parsley, if desired.

PREPARATION TIP
For a more intense bacon flavor, omit the olive oil and Canadian bacon. Use one or two strips of regular bacon. Chop the bacon and lightly brown in Step 1 before adding the vegetables.

Calories: 334 · Protein: 30 g
Fat: 8 g/21% calories from fat · Carbohydrate: 36 g
Cholesterol: 60 mg · Sodium: 790 mg

Chicken-Noodle Soup

Serves 4

- **3** CUPS CHICKEN BROTH
- **2** CUPS WATER
- **1** TEASPOON THYME
- **¼** TEASPOON PEPPER
- **4** LARGE CHICKEN THIGHS (ABOUT 1¼ POUNDS)
- **2** MEDIUM CARROTS, THINLY SLICED
- **1** CUP EGG NOODLES
- **2** CUPS PACKED FRESH SPINACH LEAVES, TORN INTO BITE-SIZE PIECES
- **1** CUP FROZEN OR CANNED, DRAINED, WHOLE-KERNEL CORN

1 In large covered saucepan, bring the chicken broth, water, thyme and pepper to a boil over high heat. Add the chicken thighs; return to a boil. Reduce the heat to medium-low, cover and simmer 10 minutes.

2 Transfer chicken thighs to a plate. Return the broth to a boil over medium-high heat. Add the carrots and noodles; cook until the noodles are al dente, about 4 to 6 minutes.

3 Meanwhile, skin the chicken thighs, remove the meat from the bone and cut the meat into bite-size pieces (it will still be slightly pink).

4 Return the chicken to the soup. Add the spinach and corn, and cook at a simmer until chicken is cooked through, about 3 minutes.

PREPARATION TIP
To eliminate having to remove the skin and bones, use already skinned and boned chicken or precut chicken strips used for stir-frying.

Calories: 213 · Protein: 22 g
Fat: 5 g/21% calories from fat · Carbohydrate: 21 g
Cholesterol: 76 mg · Sodium: 853 mg

Cock-A-Leekie Soup

Serves 6

1⅔ POUNDS POTATOES, SLICED ¼ INCH THICK
1 TABLESPOON BUTTER OR MARGARINE
2 LARGE RIBS CELERY, DICED
2 MEDIUM CARROTS, PEELED AND DICED
6 CUPS CHICKEN BROTH
1 TEASPOON SOY SAUCE
½ TEASPOON WORCESTERSHIRE SAUCE
1½ POUNDS SKINLESS, BONELESS CHICKEN BREASTS, CUT INTO ½-INCH PIECES
½ CUP ALL-PURPOSE FLOUR
½ TEASPOON ONION POWDER
SALT AND PEPPER TO TASTE
1 CUP HEAVY CREAM
⅔ CUP RAISINS

1 In large saucepan, place the potatoes and enough water to cover over high heat. Bring to a boil and cook, partially covered, just until barely tender, about 10 to 15 minutes. Drain; set aside.

2 In large saucepan or Dutch oven, heat butter until melted. Add celery and carrots; cook until tender, about 5 to 7 minutes. Add reserved potatoes, chicken broth, soy sauce and Worcestershire. Bring to a simmer over medium heat.

3 Meanwhile, dip chicken pieces into a mixture of flour, onion powder, salt and pepper until well coated. Add chicken pieces to broth-vegetable mixture. Do not stir; just push them into the liquid. Cook 20 minutes.

4 Reduce heat to low; add heavy cream and raisins. Cook until chicken is cooked through, about 20 minutes, stirring occasionally.

Calories: 550 · Protein: 36 g
Fat: 22 g/36% calories from fat · Carbohydrate: 51 g
Cholesterol: 132 mg · Sodium: 965 mg

Oriental Noodle Soup

Serves 4

5 CUPS CHICKEN BROTH
2 CUPS WATER
4 QUARTER-SIZE SLICES (¼ INCH THICK) FRESH GINGER, UNPEELED
½ TEASPOON ORIENTAL SESAME OIL
½ POUND ANGEL HAIR PASTA (CAPELLINI)
1 THICK SLICE HAM (ABOUT ¼ POUND), CUT INTO 2-INCH BY ¼-INCH STRIPS
4 LETTUCE LEAVES, SHREDDED
2 MEDIUM ZUCCHINI (ABOUT ¾ POUND), CUT INTO 2-INCH BY ¼-INCH STRIPS
4 MEDIUM CARROTS, CUT INTO 2-INCH BY ¼-INCH STRIPS

1 In large saucepan or Dutch oven, combine broth, water, ginger and sesame oil. Bring to a boil over medium-high heat.

2 Add the pasta and cook until just barely al dente, about 5 to 7 minutes.

3 Arrange the ham and vegetables on top of soup, covering one-quarter of the surface with each ingredient. Cover and cook until lettuce is wilted and ham is heated through, about 2 to 3 minutes.

PREPARATION TIP

Make this eye-appealing soup in an attractive large flameproof casserole and bring it directly to the table after cooking for a great presentation.

Calories: 332 · Protein: 17 g
Fat: 5 g/13% calories from fat · Carbohydrate: 56 g
Cholesterol: 13 mg · Sodium: 1,690 mg

Grilled Chicken Caesar Salad

The Caesar salad, so popular in the 1920s, is back and elevated to a main dish with the addition of grilled seasoned chicken.

Serves 6

- **3** CLOVES GARLIC, PEELED
- **3** TABLESPOONS OLIVE OIL, PEELED
- **1** TEASPOON GRATED LEMON PEEL
- **½** TEASPOON SALT
- **½** TEASPOON PEPPER
- **6** SLICES FRENCH BREAD
- **¾** POUND SKINLESS, BONELESS CHICKEN BREASTS
- **3** TABLESPOONS FRESH LEMON JUICE
- **6** TO 8 ANCHOVY FILLETS
- **2** TABLESPOONS MAYONNAISE
- **8** CUPS ROMAINE LETTUCE, TORN INTO BITE-SIZE PIECES
- **¼** CUP GRATED PARMESAN CHEESE

1 Prepare grill according to manufacturer's directions or preheat broiler. Spray with non-stick cooking spray.

2 Mince 1 clove garlic. In small bowl, combine minced garlic, 1 tablespoon oil, lemon peel, ¼ teaspoon salt and ¼ teaspoon pepper. Lightly brush 1 side of each bread slice with oil-lemon mixture. Rub chicken with remaining oil-lemon mixture to coat well; let stand at least 10 minutes.

3 In food processor or blender, combine remaining oil, salt and pepper, lemon juice, anchovies and mayonnaise. With the machine running, drop in remaining 2 cloves garlic; process until smooth. Place the dressing in a large salad bowl.

4 Grill or broil chicken 4 inches from heat source, turning once, until cooked through, about 8 to 10 minutes. Grill or broil bread until toasted, about 1 to 2 minutes. Cut the slices in half crosswise.

5 Cut the chicken on an angle into thin strips. Add Romaine and Parmesan to dressing; toss to coat well. Add toast and chicken; toss gently until well mixed.

PREPARATION TIP

If desired, to save time, omit the French bread, seasoning and broiling and use store-bought prepared garlic-flavored croutons.

Calories: 269 · Protein: 20 g
Fat: 11 g/39% calories from fat · Carbohydrate: 20 g
Cholesterol: 41 mg · Sodium: 487 mg

Cheddar-Chicken Chowder

Serves 4

4 TABLESPOONS BUTTER OR MARGARINE
2 GREEN ONIONS, CHOPPED
1 SMALL CLOVE GARLIC, MINCED
½ CUP ALL-PURPOSE FLOUR
2 CUPS CHICKEN BROTH
1 CUP WATER
1½ TEASPOONS DRIED THYME
¼ TEASPOON PEPPER
2 MEDIUM CARROTS, DICED
2 RIBS CELERY, DICED
1 POUND SKINLESS, BONELESS CHICKEN BREASTS, CUT INTO ½-INCH CHUNKS
1 CUP MILK
1 CUP GRATED WHITE OR YELLOW CHEDDAR CHEESE

1 In a large saucepan, melt butter over medium-high heat until warm. Add green onions and garlic and cook until the green onions have softened, about 3 minutes.

2 Add the flour and cook, stirring, until it is no longer visible, about 30 seconds. Increase the heat to medium-high and stir in the chicken broth and water. Add the thyme and pepper and bring the mixture to a boil. Reduce the heat to low; cover and simmer 10 to 15 minutes.

3 Uncover the saucepan; increase the heat to medium-high and return to a boil. Add the carrots, celery and chicken, and cook, stirring occasionally, until the chicken is cooked through, about 6 minutes.

4 Add the milk and cheese and cook until the cheese has melted, about 5 minutes.

Calories: 491 · Protein: 46 g
Fat: 26 g/47% calories from fat · Carbohydrate: 17 g
Cholesterol: 152 mg · Sodium: 834 mg

Italian Chicken Tortellini Soup

Serves 4

2 LARGE SKINLESS CHICKEN BREASTS (ABOUT 1½ POUNDS)
6 CUPS WATER
1 CAN (28 OUNCES) WHOLE TOMATOES, PEELED
2 LARGE CARROTS, PEELED AND CHOPPED
2 LARGE RIBS CELERY, CHOPPED
6 LARGE FRESH BASIL LEAVES, CHOPPED, OR 2 TEASPOONS DRIED BASIL
1 CLOVE GARLIC, CHOPPED
¼ CUP DRY RED WINE
1 TABLESPOON OLIVE OIL
SALT AND PEPPER TO TASTE
1 PACKAGE (12 OUNCES) FRESH OR FROZEN CHEESE-FILLED TORTELLINI
GRATED ROMANO CHEESE FOR GARNISH

1 In large saucepan or Dutch oven, combine chicken breasts and water; cover and bring to a boil over high heat. Reduce the heat to low and simmer until cooked through, about 20 to 25 minutes.

2 Remove chicken; when cool enough to handle, remove the meat from the bone. Cut the meat into bite-size pieces; set aside. Strain the broth. If necessary, skim off fat.

3 In a food processor or blender, purée the undrained tomatoes until smooth. Return the broth to the saucepan over medium-high heat. Add puréed tomatoes, carrots, celery, basil leaves, garlic, wine, oil, salt and pepper.

4 Reduce the heat to low and simmer, covered, until vegetables are tender, about 45 to 60 minutes. Meanwhile, cook tortellini according to package directions.

5 Add reserved chicken pieces and tortellini. Cook until heated through, about 5 to 8 minutes. Serve topped with Romano cheese.

Calories: 513 · Protein: 50 g
Fat: 13 g/24% calories from fat · Carbohydrate: 44 g
Cholesterol: 138 mg · Sodium: 740 mg

Ancho-Chicken and Sweet Corn Soup

Serves 4

8 CUPS CHICKEN BROTH
4 DRIED ANCHO PEPPERS, CHOPPED
3 LARGE TOMATOES, COARSELY CHOPPED
2 LARGE CARROTS, CHOPPED
2 MEDIUM ONIONS, CHOPPED
4 RIBS CELERY, CHOPPED
4 CLOVES GARLIC, MINCED
½ CUP MOLASSES
½ CUP FIRMLY PACKED BROWN SUGAR
½ CUP CHOPPED CILANTRO
SALT AND PEPPER TO TASTE
4 SKINLESS, BONELESS CHICKEN BREAST HALVES (ABOUT 1¼ POUNDS), GRILLED
2 CUPS HOT COOKED ARBORIO OR LONG-GRAIN RICE
1 CUP FRESH OR FROZEN WHOLE-KERNEL CORN

1 In large saucepan or Dutch oven, combine chicken broth, ancho peppers, and next 7 ingredients; cover and bring to a boil over medium-high heat. Reduce heat to low and simmer, uncovered, until reduced by half, about 45 to 60 minutes.

2 Stir in cilantro, salt and pepper. Cool slightly. In food processor or blender, with top slightly ajar, carefully purée until smooth. Strain and return to saucepan over low heat.

3 Cut chicken breasts on the diagonal into thin slices. Add sliced chicken, cooked rice and corn to broth. Cover and cook until heated through, about 2 to 3 minutes.

Calories: 691 · Protein: 49 g
Fat: 8 g/11% calories from fat · Carbohydrate: 104 g
Cholesterol: 91 mg · Sodium: 1,722 mg

Chicken Mushroom Chowder

Serves 4

3 CUPS CHICKEN BROTH
½ CUP WATER
1 POUND SKINLESS, BONELESS CHICKEN BREAST HALVES, CUT INTO 1-INCH PIECES
1½ TEASPOONS DRIED OREGANO
¼ TEASPOON PEPPER
1 TABLESPOON OLIVE OR OTHER VEGETABLE OIL
3 CLOVES GARLIC, MINCED
1 MEDIUM ONION, COARSELY CHOPPED
2 TABLESPOONS BUTTER OR MARGARINE
½ CUP LONG-GRAIN RICE
1 MEDIUM CARROT, COARSELY CHOPPED
¾ POUND MUSHROOMS, COARSELY CHOPPED
3 TABLESPOONS ALL-PURPOSE FLOUR
1 CUP MILK

1 In large saucepan or Dutch oven, combine chicken broth and water; cover and bring to a boil over high heat.

2 Add chicken, oregano and pepper. Reduce heat to medium-low; cover and simmer until chicken is cooked through, about 15 to 20 minutes. Remove chicken; set chicken and broth aside.

3 In another large saucepan or Dutch oven, heat oil over medium-high heat until hot. Add garlic and onion; cook until onion is tender, about 3 minutes. Add butter, rice, carrots and mushrooms; cook, stirring, to melt butter and coat ingredients, about 3 minutes.

4 Stir in flour; cook, stirring, about 30 seconds. Add reserved broth and bring to a boil. Reduce heat to medium-low; cover and simmer until the rice is tender, about 20 minutes.

5 Stir in chicken and milk. Cook until heated through, about 2 to 3 minutes.

Calories: 445 · Protein: 36 g
Fat: 16 g/34% calories from fat · Carbohydrate: 36 g
Cholesterol: 96 mg · Sodium: 734 mg

Chicken Goulash Soup

Serves 6

2 TEASPOONS OLIVE OIL
3 MEDIUM ONIONS, THINLY SLICED
2 MEDIUM GREEN PEPPERS, CUT INTO ¾-INCH PIECES
2 TABLESPOONS PAPRIKA, PREFERABLY HUNGARIAN
¼ TEASPOON CUMIN
¼ TEASPOON PEPPER
8 CUPS CHICKEN BROTH
2 TABLESPOONS CORNSTARCH
¼ POUND WIDE EGG NOODLES, COOKED
1 POUND SKINLESS, BONELESS CHICKEN BREAST HALVES, CUT ACROSS THE GRAIN INTO THIN STRIPS
¼ TEASPOON SALT

1 In large saucepan or Dutch oven, heat the oil over medium heat. Add the onions; cook, stirring frequently, until browned, about 15 minutes.

2 Stir in peppers, paprika, cumin, pepper and 7¾ cups broth. In small bowl, stir remaining ¼ cup broth and cornstarch until smooth; pour into saucepan. Bring to a boil. Reduce heat to low; simmer, partially covered, about 20 minutes.

3 Cook noodles according to package directions; drain and set aside.

4 Add chicken strips to broth; simmer, covered, until chicken is cooked through, about 3 to 4 minutes. Add noodles; cook until heated through, about 2 minutes.

Calories: 264 · Protein: 27 g
Fat: 7 g/24% calories from fat · Carbohydrate: 21 g
Cholesterol: 65 mg · Sodium: 1,170 mg

Turkey-Soba Soup

Serves 4

4 CUPS CHICKEN BROTH
2 CUPS WATER
3 MEDIUM CARROTS, CUT INTO MATCHSTICK PIECES
1 MEDIUM RED ONION, CUT INTO THIN WEDGES
3 QUARTER-SIZE SLICES (¼ INCH THICK) FRESH GINGER, PEELED, MINCED
½ POUND SOBA NOODLES
½ POUND FRESH SPINACH OR 1 PACKAGE (10 OUNCES) FROZEN LEAF SPINACH, THAWED
¼ CUP CHOPPED CILANTRO (OPTIONAL)
2 TEASPOONS ORIENTAL SESAME OIL
¼ TEASPOON PEPPER
8 OUNCES COOKED CHICKEN BREAST, CUT INTO ½-INCH-WIDE STRIPS
2 TEASPOONS SESAME SEEDS, TOASTED

1 In large saucepan or Dutch oven, combine chicken broth and water. Bring to a boil over medium-high heat. Add the carrots, onion and ginger. Reduce heat to low; cover and simmer about 5 minutes.

2 Increase heat to medium-high and bring to a boil, uncovered. Add noodles until al dente, about 5 to 8 minutes. A minute before noodles are done, add spinach, cilantro, if desired, sesame oil and pepper. Cook until noodles are done and spinach is wilted.

3 Serve broth, noodles and vegetables topped with chicken strips and sesame seeds.

PREPARATION TIP
Soba noodles are found in Asian markets or in the international food section of large supermarkets. They are made of buckwheat, which gives them a hearty, nutty flavor and firm texture. Use thick spaghetti or fettucine if you can't find them.

Calories: 286 · Protein: 27 g
Fat: 8 g/26% calories from fat · Carbohydrate: 25 g
Cholesterol: 66 mg · Sodium: 885 mg

Hot-and-Sour Chicken Soup

Traditionally made with pork and exotic dried mushrooms, this hearty soup from the cold northern provinces of China is a spicy, lighter version.

Serves 4

- **3** CUPS CHICKEN BROTH
- **½** CUP WATER
- **¼** POUND SMALL MUSHROOMS
- **½** CUP CANNED SLICED BAMBOO SHOOTS
- **3** QUARTER-SIZE SLICES (¼ INCH THICK) FRESH GINGER, UNPEELED
- **2** CLOVES GARLIC, MINCED
- **2** TEASPOONS REDUCED-SODIUM SOY SAUCE
- **¼** TEASPOON RED PEPPER FLAKES
- **1** POUND SKINLESS, BONELESS CHICKEN BREASTS
- **1** TABLESPOON ORIENTAL SESAME OIL
- **3** TABLESPOONS RED WINE VINEGAR OR CIDER VINEGAR
- **2** TABLESPOONS CORNSTARCH
- **1** EGG
- **2** GREEN ONIONS WITH TOPS, FINELY CHOPPED
- **¼** CUP CILANTRO SPRIGS, FINELY CHOPPED (OPTIONAL)

1 In medium covered saucepan, bring the chicken broth, water, mushrooms, bamboo shoots, ginger, garlic, soy sauce and red pepper flakes to a boil over medium-high heat. Reduce the heat to low, cover and simmer 10 to 15 minutes.

2 Meanwhile, slice chicken across the grain into ¼-inch-thick pieces. Place chicken pieces in a bowl and toss them with sesame oil.

3 In small bowl, blend the vinegar and cornstarch until well combined. In another small bowl, lightly beat the egg.

4 Increase the heat under the broth to medium-high and return to a boil. Add the chicken pieces to the saucepan. Stirring constantly, slowly pour in the beaten egg. Stir in the vinegar mixture. Cook, stirring occasionally, until the chicken is cooked through and the soup has thickened slightly, about 3 minutes.

5 Stir in the green onions and serve sprinkled with cilantro, if desired. Remove ginger slices before serving.

PREPARATION TIP

Cut, chop and slice all the ingredients ahead of time and this main-dish soup can be made in 25 minutes or less.

Calories: 228 · Protein: 31 g
Fat: 7 g/27% calories from fat · Carbohydrate: 8 g
Cholesterol: 119 mg · Sodium: 933 mg

Lemon-Honey Chicken Skewers

Serves 4

- **3** TABLESPOONS FRESH LEMON JUICE
- **1** TABLESPOON HONEY
- **1** TABLESPOON VEGETABLE OIL
- **1** TEASPOON SOY SAUCE
- **¼** TEASPOON GROUND GINGER
- **4** SKINLESS, BONELESS CHICKEN BREAST HALVES (ABOUT 1¼ POUNDS), CUT INTO THICK STRIPS

1 In shallow bowl, combine the lemon juice, honey, oil, soy sauce and ginger.

2 Add the chicken strips, toss to coat well and let stand for at least 10 minutes.

3 Meanwhile, prepare grill according to manufacturer's directions or preheat broiler.

4 Remove chicken strips from the marinade, reserving remaining marinade, and thread them onto skewers (about 3 strips will fit on an 8-inch skewer); place them on the grill or broiler pan. Cook the chicken 4 inches from the heat source for 4 minutes. Brush with remaining marinade. Turn the skewers over and cook until the chicken is cooked through and golden, about 4 minutes.

PREPARATION TIP
This can also be made with turkey cutlets. Make them ahead and serve sliced with vegetables for a cold dinner or on top of a chef or Caesar salad.

Calories: 209 · Protein: 28 g
Fat: 7 g/33% calories from fat · Carbohydrate: 5 g
Cholesterol: 77 mg · Sodium: 157 mg

Oven-Baked Chicken Nuggets

Serves 4

- **2** CLOVES GARLIC, COARSELY CHOPPED
- **¼** CUP PARSLEY SPRIGS (OPTIONAL)
- **4** SLICES DAY-OLD, WHOLEWHEAT OR WHITE BREAD, TORN INTO SMALL PIECES
- **¼** CUP GRATED PARMESAN CHEESE
- **½** TEASPOON SALT
- **½** TEASPOON PEPPER
- **2** TABLESPOONS CHILLED BUTTER, CUT INTO SMALL PIECES
- **2** TABLESPOONS MILK
- **1** POUND SKINLESS, BONELESS CHICKEN BREASTS, CUT INTO 1-INCH CUBES

1 Preheat oven to 425°. Line a baking sheet with foil and grease lightly; set aside.

2 In food processor or blender, finely chop garlic and parsley, if desired. Add bread, Parmesan cheese, salt and pepper. Process, pulsing machine on and off, until bread is coarsely crumbled.

3 Add butter and process until butter is completely incorporated. Transfer the breading to a paper or plastic bag. Place milk in small bowl. Add chicken; toss to coat well. Drain off any excess milk.

4 Place milk-coated chicken in bag of breading and shake until well coated.

5 Place coated nuggets on the prepared baking sheet, spaced apart. Bake until crisp and browned, about 12 to 15 minutes, turning halfway through.

PREPARATION TIP
The breading mixture can be made ahead and kept in the refrigerator until it's ready to be used. The nuggets can also be breaded well ahead and frozen.

Calories: 309 · Protein: 32 g
Fat: 13 g/38% calories from fat · Carbohydrate: 15 g
Cholesterol: 92 mg · Sodium: 687 mg

Buffalo Chicken Fingers

Lean chicken breast is substituted for the usual wings to keep the calories and fat to a minimum.

Serves 4

½ CUP LOW-FAT (1%) MILK
½ TEASPOON HONEY
1 POUND SKINLESS, BONELESS CHICKEN BREASTS, CUT INTO 1-INCH-WIDE STRIPS
1 CUP CRUSHED CORNFLAKES (ABOUT 2 CUPS UNCRUSHED)
¼ TEASPOON GROUND GINGER
¼ TEASPOON DRIED THYME
¼ TEASPOON DRIED ROSEMARY
1 CUP PLAIN YOGURT
2 OUNCES BLUE CHEESE, CRUMBLED
4 GREEN ONIONS, MINCED
6 DROPS HOT PEPPER SAUCE
2 CARROTS, CUT INTO MATCHSTICK PIECES
2 RIBS CELERY, CUT INTO MATCHSTICK PIECES

1 Preheat oven to 400°. Line baking pan with foil and spray with nonstick cooking spray. Set aside.

2 In shallow bowl, combine milk and honey until well mixed. Add chicken strips; toss to evenly coat. Let stand 10 minutes.

3 In plastic or paper bag or shallow dish, combine cornflakes, ginger, thyme and rosemary until well mixed. Add chicken strips; toss to evenly coat and gently press to coat.

4 Place on prepared baking pan. Bake until crisp, golden and cooked through, about 8 minutes.

5 Meanwhile, to make dressing, in medium bowl, combine yogurt, blue cheese, green onions and hot pepper sauce until well mixed.

6 Serve chicken strips with blue cheese dressing and carrot and celery matchstick pieces.

PREPARATION TIP

To crush cornflakes, place them in a resealable plastic bag; seal, and run a rolling pin or heavy glass over the bag.

Calories: 357 · Protein: 37 g
Fat: 6 g/ 15% calories from fat · Carbohydrate: 37 g
Cholesterol: 79 mg · Sodium: 716 mg

Chicken Porcupines

Serves 4

4 GREEN ONIONS
3 CLOVES GARLIC
3 QUARTER-SIZE SLICES (¼ INCH THICK) FRESH GINGER, PEELED
¼ CUP CILANTRO SPRIGS
1 POUND GROUND CHICKEN
¼ CUP LONG-GRAIN RICE
1 EGG
½ TEASPOON SALT
¼ TEASPOON PEPPER
1 TABLESPOON OLIVE OIL
1 CUP CHICKEN BROTH
½ CUP CANNED CRUSHED TOMATOES
1 TABLESPOON CORNSTARCH

1 In food processor or blender, process the green onions, garlic, ginger and cilantro until finely chopped.

2 In medium bowl, combine the ground chicken, rice, egg, salt, pepper and half of green onion-garlic mixture. Mix gently until well combined. Using about 2 tablespoons chicken mixture for each, form the mixture into balls.

3 In large skillet, heat oil over medium-high heat. Add the remaining green onion-garlic mixture and cook, stirring frequently, until lightly browned, about 3 minutes.

4 Add ¾ cup broth and tomatoes; bring to a boil. Add the chicken balls. Reduce heat to low; cover and simmer, stirring occasionally, until rice is cooked, about 20 minutes.

5 In small bowl, combine the remaining ¼ cup broth with cornstarch until well blended.

6 Increase heat to high; uncover and bring back to a boil. Add broth-cornstarch mixture; cook, stirring constantly, until thickened slightly, about 1 minute.

Calories: 321 · Protein: 25 g
Fat: 16 g/45% calories from fat · Carbohydrate: 18 g
Cholesterol: 175 mg · Sodium: 287 mg

Honey-Soy Chicken

Serves 4

3 TABLESPOONS REDUCED-SODIUM SOY SAUCE
1 TABLESPOON HONEY
3 CLOVES GARLIC, MINCED
3 QUARTER-SIZE SLICES (¼ INCH THICK) FRESH GINGER, UNPEELED
¼ TEASPOON PEPPER
4 SKINLESS, BONELESS CHICKEN BREAST HALVES (ABOUT 1¼ POUNDS)
1 TEASPOON SESAME SEEDS, TOASTED (OPTIONAL)
HOT COOKED RICE (OPTIONAL)

1 In shallow bowl, combine soy sauce, honey, garlic, ginger slices and pepper.

2 Cut the chicken lengthwise into thin strips. Place the chicken in the marinade and toss to coat well.

3 Preheat broiler. Line broiler pan with foil.

4 Remove chicken strips from the marinade, thread them onto skewers (about 3 strips will fit on an 8-inch skewer) and place them on the broiler pan. Broil the chicken 4 inches from heat source for 4 minutes. Turn the skewers over and broil until the chicken is cooked through and golden, about 4 minutes.

5 Sprinkle with sesame seeds and serve over rice, if desired.

PREPARATION TIP
For do-ahead ease, cut the chicken and marinate in refrigerator for several hours or even overnight.

Calories: 345 · Protein: 36 g
Fat: 5 g/13% calories from fat · Carbohydrate: 35 g
Cholesterol: 82 mg · Sodium: 419 mg

Chicken Tortilla Soup

This Mexican-style soup is not only easy, hearty, flavorful and attractive, it also makes a great winter meal.

Serves 4

- **1** MEDIUM ONION, COARSELY CHOPPED, DIVIDED
- **3** CLOVES GARLIC, MINCED, DIVIDED
- **⅓** CUP FINELY CHOPPED CILANTRO, DIVIDED
- **1** TABLESPOON PLUS 2 TEASPOONS OIL
- **2** TEASPOONS CUMIN, DIVIDED
- **1½** TEASPOONS DRIED OREGANO, DIVIDED
- **½** TEASPOON PEPPER, DIVIDED
- **½** POUND SKINLESS, BONELESS CHICKEN BREASTS
- **2** CUPS CHICKEN BROTH
- **1** CUP WATER
- **1** CAN (14½ OUNCES) NO-SALT-ADDED STEWED TOMATOES
- **1** CUP TOMATO JUICE
- **2** TEASPOONS LIME ZEST
- **2** TABLESPOONS LIME JUICE
- **½** TEASPOON WORCESTERSHIRE SAUCE
- **1** FRESH OR PICKLED JALAPEÑO PEPPER, SEEDED AND MINCED
- **4** SMALL CORN TORTILLAS, CUT CROSSWISE INTO STRIPS, TOASTED
- **½** CUP SHREDDED MONTEREY JACK CHEESE (2 OUNCES)

1 Preheat the broiler. In small bowl combine half the onion, garlic and cilantro. Stir in the 1 tablespoon oil, ½ teaspoon of the oregano and ¼ teaspoon pepper.

2 Place the chicken on a broiler pan and top with onion-herb mixture. Broil 4-inches from heat source, 7 minutes. Turn; baste with any pan juices and broil until cooked through, about 7 to 9 minutes. Cool; then pull apart into shreds.

3 Meanwhile, in a medium saucepan, heat the remaining 2 teaspoons oil over medium-high heat. Add the remaining onion and garlic; cook, stirring, until the onion is lightly browned, about 3 to 4 minutes.

4 Add broth, water, tomatoes, tomato juice, lime zest and juice, Worcestershire sauce and remaining cilantro, cumin, oregano and pepper. Bring to a boil and reduce heat to low; cover and simmer 7 minutes. Stir in jalapeño.

5 To serve, ladle soup into bowls and top with chicken, tortilla strips and cheese.

PREPARATION TIP

To toast tortilla strips, place on baking sheet and bake in preheated 400° oven until toasted, about 7 minutes.

Calories: 291 · Protein: 22 g
Fat: 13 g/42% calories from fat · Carbohydrate: 20 g
Cholesterol: 49 mg · Sodium: 730 mg

Hot and Spicy Buffalo Wings

Serves 4

- VEGETABLE OIL FOR FRYING
- **2** POUNDS CHICKEN WINGS, CUT INTO 2 PIECES AT JOINT
- SALT AND PEPPER TO TASTE
- **4** TABLESPOONS BUTTER OR MARGARINE
- **4** TABLESPOONS HOT PEPPER SAUCE
- **1** TABLESPOON WHITE WINE VINEGAR
- **2** RIBS CELERY, CUT INTO MATCHSTICK PIECES
- **1** CUP BLUE CHEESE SALAD DRESSING

1 In a deep-fryer or deep skillet, heat about 2 inches oil to 375°. Pat chicken wings dry and season them with salt and pepper.

2 Carefully lower a few wings into oil. Fry, turning occasionally, until golden and crisp, about 10 to 12 minutes. Remove and drain on paper towels. Transfer to large bowl.

3 In a small saucepan, heat butter over medium-low heat until melted. Stir in hot pepper sauce and vinegar. Pour over fried wings; toss to coat well.

4 Arrange chicken wings on serving plate with blue cheese dressing and celery sticks.

PREPARATION TIP

Arrange the wings in small batches to avoid overcrowding the pan and uneven browning.

Calories: 1,090 · Protein: 85 g
Fat: 76 g/64% calories from fat · Carbohydrate: 13 g
Cholesterol: 321 mg · Sodium: 423 mg

Southern-Fried Chicken Strips

Serves 4

- **⅓** CUP ALL-PURPOSE FLOUR
- **2** TABLESPOONS CHOPPED PARSLEY (OPTIONAL)
- **1** TEASPOON PAPRIKA
- **½** TEASPOON SALT
- **¼** TEASPOON PEPPER
- DASH OF CAYENNE PEPPER
- **4** SKINLESS, BONELESS CHICKEN BREAST HALVES (ABOUT 1¼ POUNDS), CUT ACROSS THE GRAIN INTO ½-INCH-WIDE STRIPS
- **2** TABLESPOONS PLUS 1 TEASPOON VEGETABLE OIL
- **¼** CUP DIJON OR WHOLE-GRAIN MUSTARD
- **1½** TEASPOONS HONEY
- **1** TEASPOON CIDER VINEGAR

1 In plastic or paper bag, combine flour, parsley, if desired, paprika, salt and peppers. Add the chicken strips and shake to coat lightly.

2 In large nonstick skillet, heat 2 tablespoons oil over medium-high heat until hot. Add the chicken strips in one layer; cook, turning frequently, until cooked through and golden, about 7 minutes. Drain the chicken on paper towels.

3 In small bowl, stir the remaining 1 teaspoon oil, mustard, honey and vinegar until well combined. Serve with chicken.

Calories: 331 · Protein: 35 g
Fat: 13 g/38% calories from fat · Carbohydrate: 15 g
Cholesterol: 89 mg · Sodium: 545 mg

Moroccan-Spiced Chicken Salad

Made with a grain called couscous, which is a staple used in North African cuisine, this granular semolina comes precooked in packages available in Middle-Eastern markets and international sections in large supermarkets.

Serves 4

- **1** TEASPOON PAPRIKA
- **¾** TEASPOON SALT
- **2** SKINLESS, BONELESS CHICKEN BREAST HALVES (ABOUT ¾ POUND)
- **1** CUP COUSCOUS
- **2½** CUPS BOILING WATER
- **2** CUPS COLD WATER
- **¾** TEASPOON GROUND GINGER
- **½** TEASPOON GROUND CORIANDER
- **¼** TEASPOON CINNAMON
- **3** CARROTS, HALVED LENGTHWISE AND THINLY SLICED
- **2** GREEN PEPPERS, CUT INTO 1-INCH PIECES
- **1** LARGE TOMATO, FINELY CHOPPED
- **4** TEASPOONS OLIVE OR OTHER VEGETABLE OIL
- **1** TABLESPOON HONEY
- **¼** TEASPOON PEPPER
- **⅓** CUP CHOPPED FRESH CILANTRO OR PARSLEY

1 Preheat broiler. Combine ½ teaspoon paprika and ¼ teaspoon salt; rub over chicken. Place chicken on broiler pan. Broil 6 inches from heat source until lightly browned, about 4 to 6 minutes. Turn and broil until cooked through, about 4 to 6 minutes. Remove and cool slightly; cut into 1-inch cubes. Set aside.

2 In medium bowl, combine couscous and boiling water. Cover and let stand until couscous has softened and water is absorbed, about 5 to 10 minutes.

3 Meanwhile, in large skillet, combine cold water, ginger, cumin, coriander and cinnamon. Bring to a boil over medium heat. Add carrots; cook until crisp-tender, about 4 minutes. Add green peppers; cook until crisp-tender, about 1 minute. Transfer carrots and green peppers to large bowl; reserve ¼ cup cooking liquid.

4 To cooked carrots and peppers add remaining ½ teaspoon paprika and ½ teaspoon salt, tomato, oil, honey, pepper and reserved cooking liquid; toss gently to evenly coat.

5 Add chicken, couscous and cilantro; toss gently to evenly coat.

PREPARATION TIP

This salad can be made up to 8 hours in advance and served chilled or at room temperature.

Calories: 368 · Protein: 27 g
Fat: 6 g/15% calories from fat · Carbohydrate: 50 g
Cholesterol: 49 mg · Sodium: 497 mg

Curried Chicken Salad

Serves 4

- **¼** CUP REDUCED-FAT MAYONNAISE
- **¼** CUP PLAIN YOGURT
- **1** TABLESPOON ORANGE MARMALADE, APRICOT JAM OR MANGO CHUTNEY
- **2** TEASPOONS CURRY POWDER
- **⅛** TEASPOON SALT
- **⅛** TEASPOON PEPPER
- **8** OUNCES COOKED CHICKEN, CUT INTO ½-INCH CUBES (ABOUT 1½ CUPS)
- **1** GRANNY SMITH APPLE OR OTHER TART GREEN APPLE, CORED, CUT INTO ½-INCH PIECES
- **1** CUP SEEDLESS RED GRAPES
- **½** CUP WALNUT OR PECAN PIECES

1 To make dressing, in medium serving bowl, combine mayonnaise, yogurt, marmalade, curry powder, salt and pepper until well mixed.

2 To dressing add chicken, apple, grapes and walnuts; toss to evenly coat.

PREPARATION TIP
A great way to use leftover chicken or even substitute turkey around holiday time.

Calories: 294 · Protein: 20 g
Fat: 18 g/ 55% calories from fat · Carbohydrate: 18 g
Cholesterol: 49 mg · Sodium: 205 mg

Garlic-Dressed Spinach and Artichoke Salad

Serves 4

- **8** OUNCES FRESH SPINACH, TRIMMED, WASHED, TORN INTO BITE-SIZE PIECES
- **3½** CUPS SHREDDED RED CABBAGE (ABOUT 8 OUNCES)
- **1** LARGE YELLOW OR GREEN PEPPER, CUT INTO ¼-INCH-WIDE STRIPS
- **1** CAN (14 OUNCES) ARTICHOKE HEARTS, DRAINED, HALVED IF LARGE
- **8** OUNCES COOKED CHICKEN, CUT INTO ½-INCH CUBES
- **1** CUP MAYONNAISE
- **2** TABLESPOONS LEMON JUICE
- **2** TEASPOONS WORCESTERSHIRE SAUCE
- **3** CLOVES GARLIC, PEELED AND BRUISED

1 In large salad bowl, combine spinach, red cabbage, yellow pepper, artichoke hearts and chicken; set aside.

2 To make dressing, in small bowl, combine mayonnaise, lemon juice and Worcestershire sauce until well mixed. Add bruised garlic. Cover and refrigerate until ready to serve (the longer the garlic sits, the stronger the garlic flavor). Remove garlic before serving.

3 To serve, add dressing to chicken-vegetable mixture; toss gently to evenly coat.

PREPARATION TIP
If canned artichokes are not available, substitute 2 jars (6 ounces each) and drain well.

Calories: 568 · Protein: 23 g
Fat: 47 g/72% calories from fat · Carbohydrate: 16 g
Cholesterol: 80 mg · Sodium: 503 mg

Grilled Chicken and Orange Salad

Serves 4

1 POUND SMALL RED POTATOES, CUT IN HALF
8 OUNCES FRESH GREEN BEANS
¼ CUP ORANGE JUICE
2 TABLESPOON ORANGE MARMALADE
2 TABLESPOONS MAPLE SYRUP
½ TEASPOON SALT
½ TEASPOON GRATED ORANGE PEEL
½ TEASPOON GINGER
¼ TEASPOON PEPPER
2 SMALL SKINLESS, BONELESS CHICKEN BREAST HALVES (ABOUT 1 POUND)
1 TABLESPOON RED WINE VINEGAR
2 TEASPOONS DIJON MUSTARD
4 CUPS TORN RED LEAF LETTUCE
2 LARGE ORANGES, PEELED AND SECTIONED

1 Preheat broiler or grill according to manufacturer's directions.

2 In medium saucepan, place potatoes and enough water to cover over high heat. Bring to a boil and cook, just until tender, about 10 minutes. Add green beans during last 2 minutes. Drain.

3 In large bowl, combine orange juice, marmalade, maple syrup, salt, orange peel, ginger and pepper until well mixed. Remove ¼ cup orange mixture for basting chicken.

4 Brush chicken with reserved orange mixture. Broil or grill 4 inches from heat source until lightly browned, about 8 to 12 minutes, brushing with orange mixture. Remove chicken and cool slightly; cut across the grain into ¼-inch-thick slices. Set aside.

5 To remaining orange mixture add vinegar and mustard until well mixed. Add potatoes, green beans, chicken, lettuce and orange sections; toss gently to evenly coat.

Calories: 357 · Protein: 32 g
Fat: 4 g/11% calories from fat · Carbohydrate: 48 g
Cholesterol: 71 mg · Sodium: 392 mg

Chicken Taco Salad

Serves 4

⅔ CUP MILD RED SALSA
½ CUP SOUR CREAM
1 TABLESPOON CUMIN
¾ TEASPOON SALT
½ TEASPOON PEPPER
1 CAN (15½ TO 19 OUNCES) KIDNEY BEANS, RINSED AND DRAINED
1 CAN (16 OUNCES) WHOLE-KERNEL CORN, DRAINED
8 OUNCES COOKED CHICKEN, CUT INTO ½-INCH CUBES (ABOUT 2 CUPS)
3 RIBS CELERY, CUT INTO ½-INCH PIECES
8 LETTUCE LEAVES, SHREDDED
2 CUPS UNSALTED TORTILLA CHIPS

1 To make dressing, in small serving bowl, combine salsa, sour cream, cumin, salt and pepper until well mixed.

2 In large bowl, combine beans, corn, chicken and celery; toss until mixed.

3 To serve, arrange a bed of lettuce on each plate; top with chicken-bean mixture and salsa. Garnish with tortilla chips.

PREPARATION TIP
This is a great do-ahead meal. Mix the salsa, toss the beans, corn, chicken and celery; then cover and refrigerate until serving time. Shred the lettuce, arrange on the plates and add the chips on the side. The tortilla chips should not be added until the last moment or they will get soggy.

Calories: 454 · Protein: 25 g
Fat: 17 g/33% calories from fat · Carbohydrate: 53 g
Cholesterol: 56 mg · Sodium: 939 mg

Spanish Chicken-Rice Salad

Serves 4

- **2¼** CUPS WATER
- **1** CUP LONG-GRAIN RICE
- **¾** TEASPOON SALT
- **1** CUP REDUCED-SODIUM CHICKEN BROTH, FAT REMOVED
- **2** CLOVES GARLIC, MINCED
- **¼** TEASPOON PEPPER
- **⅛** TEASPOON SAFFRON OR ¼ TEASPOON TURMERIC
- **2** SKINLESS, BONELESS CHICKEN BREAST HALVES (ABOUT ¾ POUND)
- **1** CUP FROZEN PEAS
- **¼** CUP FRESH LEMON JUICE
- **1** TABLESPOON EXTRA-VIRGIN OLIVE OIL
- **1** RED PEPPER, CUT INTO ½-INCH PIECES
- **1** RED ONION, CUT INTO ½-INCH CUBES
- **2** TABLESPOONS SLIVERED ALMONDS
- **4** CUPS MIXED TORN GREENS

1 In medium saucepan, bring water to a boil. Add rice and ¼ teaspoon salt. Reduce heat to low; cover and simmer until rice is tender, about 17 minutes. Place in large bowl; fluff with fork and set aside.

2 In medium skillet, combine the broth, garlic, pepper and saffron over medium heat. Bring to a boil. Reduce heat to low; cover and simmer until chicken is cooked, about 10 minutes, turning once. Add peas during last minute of cooking. Remove chicken and peas and cool slightly; cut chicken into 1-inch cubes. Set aside. Strain broth and reserve.

3 In large bowl, combine 1 cup reserved broth, lemon juice, oil and remaining ½ teaspoon salt. Add reserved rice, peas, chicken, red pepper, onion and almonds; toss gently until well mixed.

4 To serve, spoon chicken-rice mixture over greens.

Calories: 388 · Protein: 28 g
Fat: 7 g/16% calories from fat · Carbohydrate: 52 g
Cholesterol: 49 mg · Sodium: 663 mg

Honey-Mustard Chicken

Serves 4

- **3** TABLESPOONS BROWN MUSTARD
- **2** TABLESPOONS HONEY
- **1** TABLESPOON VEGETABLE OIL
- **4** TEASPOONS CIDER VINEGAR
- **1** SMALL ZUCCHINI, CUT INTO ½-INCH COINS
- **½** SMALL RED PEPPER, CUT INTO 1-INCH SQUARES
- **1** SMALL TOMATO, FINELY DICED
- **2** GREEN ONIONS, FINELY CHOPPED
- **⅛** TEASPOON PEPPER
- **4** SKINLESS, BONELESS CHICKEN BREAST HALVES (ABOUT 1¼ POUNDS)

1 Prepare broiler or grill according to manufacturer's directions.

2 In 1-cup measure, combine mustard, honey, vegetable oil and vinegar until well mixed. Place ¼ cup mustard-honey mixture in medium bowl. Add zucchini, red pepper, tomato, green onions and pepper; toss gently to evenly coat.

3 Brush chicken with remaining mustard-honey mixture. Broil or grill 4 inches from heat source until lightly browned, about 4 to 6 minutes. Turn and broil or grill until cooked through, about 4 to 6 minutes.

4 Serve chicken topped with vegetable mixture.

PREPARATION TIP
If desired, cucumbers can be substituted for zucchini. Try this sauce over pork chops or hamburgers.

Calories: 268 · Protein: 34 g
Fat: 8 g/30% calories from fat · Carbohydrate: 12 g
Cholesterol: 89 mg · Sodium: 232 mg

Chicken Breasts with Tomato-Basil Mayonnaise

Serves 4

2 PLUM TOMATOES, SEEDED AND DICED
½ TEASPOON SALT
3 CUPS WATER
1 CUP DRY WHITE WINE OR WATER
½ CUP CHOPPED CELERY
10 SPRIGS PARSLEY
2 GREEN ONIONS, SPLIT LENGTHWISE
¼ TEASPOON PEPPERCORNS
4 SKINLESS, BONELESS CHICKEN BREAST HALVES (ABOUT 1¼ POUNDS)
⅔ CUP REDUCED-FAT MAYONNAISE
2 TABLESPOONS CHOPPED FRESH OR 2 TEASPOONS DRIED BASIL
1 TEASPOON FRESH LEMON JUICE
¼ TEASPOON CAYENNE PEPPER
2 MEDIUM TOMATOES, SLICED

1 In colander, place diced tomatoes; sprinkle with salt. Let stand to drain.

2 Meanwhile, in large saucepan or skillet, combine water, wine, celery, parsley, green onions and peppercorns. Bring to a boil over medium-high heat. Add chicken. Reduce heat to low; partially cover and simmer until chicken is cooked through, about 12 to 17 minutes. Drain. Remove and cool slightly; cut across the grain into ¼-inch-thick slices. Set aside.

3 On paper towels pat tomatoes dry; place in small bowl. Add mayonnaise, basil, lemon juice and cayenne until well mixed, crushing tomatoes slightly with fork.

4 Serve sliced chicken in center of plates topped with tomato-mayonnaise mixture and surrounded with sliced tomatoes.

Calories: 378 · Protein: 34 g
Fat: 18 g/43% calories from fat · Carbohydrate: 8 g
Cholesterol: 103 mg · Sodium: 671 mg

Tarragon Chicken-Cucumber Salad

Serves 4

½ CUP CHICKEN BROTH
2 TABLESPOONS MINCED FRESH OR 1½ TEASPOONS DRIED TARRAGON
2 CLOVES GARLIC, MINCED
¼ TEASPOON PEPPER
¾ POUND SKINLESS, BONELESS CHICKEN BREASTS, THINLY SLICED ACROSS GRAIN
⅓ CUP PLAIN LOW-FAT YOGURT
1 TABLESPOON OLIVE OR OTHER VEGETABLE OIL
1 TABLESPOON RICE WINE OR WHITE WINE VINEGAR
½ TEASPOON SALT
1 MEDIUM CUCUMBER, CUBED
1 LARGE RED PEPPER, COARSELY CHOPPED
8 LETTUCE LEAVES (OPTIONAL)

1 In medium saucepan, combine broth, 1 tablespoon tarragon, garlic and pepper. Bring to a boil over medium-high heat. Add chicken. Reduce heat to low; cover and simmer, stirring occasionally, until chicken is cooked through, about 6 to 9 minutes. Remove and cool slightly; set aside. (Reserve cooking liquid for another use.)

2 To make dressing, in small bowl, combine remaining tarragon, yogurt, oil, vinegar and salt until well mixed.

3 In large serving bowl, combine cooked chicken, cucumber, red pepper and yogurt dressing; toss gently to evenly coat. Serve over lettuce, if desired.

Calories: 182 · Protein: 22 g
Fat: 7 g/35% calories from fat · Carbohydrate: 6 g
Cholesterol: 55 mg · Sodium: 436 mg

Pasta Twists with Chicken and Garlic-Pepper Cream

Serves 4

½ CUP CHICKEN BROTH
3 MEDIUM CARROTS, CUT INTO 2-INCH BY ¼-INCH STRIPS
3 CLOVES GARLIC, PEELED
8 OUNCES PASTA TWISTS* (ABOUT 2 CUPS)
1 PACKAGE (8 OUNCES) CREAM CHEESE
2 TABLESPOONS GRATED PARMESAN CHEESE
½ TEASPOON SALT
½ TEASPOON PEPPER
2 TABLESPOONS MILK
8 OUNCES COOKED CHICKEN, CUT INTO CUBES (ABOUT 1½ CUPS)
1 BUNCH GREEN ONIONS (ABOUT 6 TO 8), COARSELY CHOPPED

1 In medium saucepan, place chicken broth over medium-high heat. Bring to a boil. Add carrots and garlic. Reduce heat to medium-low; cover and cook, about 5 minutes. Drain carrots and garlic; reserve the broth.

2 Cook pasta according to package directions.

3 In food processor or blender, process cooked garlic until finely chopped. Add reserved chicken broth, cream cheese, Parmesan cheese, salt and pepper. Process until smooth, about 5 to 10 seconds. With machine running, add milk and process until smooth.

4 Drain pasta; while still hot, toss with garlic-cream cheese mixture, carrots, chicken and green onions. Serve hot.

*fusilli, rotini, rotelle

Calories: 594 · Protein: 27 g
Fat: 27 g/40% calories from fat · Carbohydrate: 53 g
Cholesterol: 128 mg · Sodium: 699 mg

Piquant Lemon Chicken Salad

Serves 4

2 SMALL SKINLESS, BONELESS CHICKEN BREAST HALVES (ABOUT 1 POUND)
¼ CUP PLAIN LOW-FAT YOGURT
¼ CUP FRESH LEMON JUICE
2 TABLESPOONS REDUCED-FAT MAYONNAISE
2 TEASPOONS GRATED LEMON PEEL
1½ TEASPOONS DRIED CORIANDER
½ TEASPOON SALT
¼ TEASPOON PEPPER
¼ TEASPOON CAYENNE PEPPER
4 GREEN ONIONS, FINELY CHOPPED
3 SLICES ¼-INCH-THICK FRESH GINGER, PEELED, MINCED
¼ CUP PARSLEY SPRIGS, FINELY CHOPPED (OPTIONAL)
1 LARGE CARROT, FINELY CHOPPED
1 LARGE GREEN PEPPER, CUT INTO THIN STRIPS
1 PINT CHERRY TOMATOES, HALVED

1 Place chicken in steamer basket over boiling water over medium heat. Reduce heat to medium-low and steam until chicken is done, about 8 to 10 minutes. Remove and cool slightly; shred and set aside.

2 In large serving bowl, combine yogurt, lemon juice, mayonnaise, lemon peel, coriander, salt, pepper and cayenne.

3 Add green onions, ginger, parsley, if desired, carrot, green pepper and cherry tomatoes; toss gently to evenly coat.

4 Add shredded chicken; toss gently to evenly coat.

Calories: 220 · Protein: 28 g
Fat: 6 g/28% calories from fat · Carbohydrate: 10 g
Cholesterol: 75 mg · Sodium: 415 mg

Mexican Chicken Salad

Serves 4

- **2** MEDIUM CARROTS, DICED
- **1½** POUNDS COOKED CHICKEN BREASTS, CUT INTO THIN STRIPS
- **1** SMALL HEAD CABBAGE, SHREDDED
- **2** BUNCHES (ABOUT 2 CUPS) FRESH CILANTRO, COARSELY CHOPPED
- **½** CUP FRESH LIME JUICE
- **½** CUP OLIVE OIL
- **1** CLOVE GARLIC, MINCED
- **½** TEASPOON CAYENNE PEPPER
- **½** TEASPOON SALT
- HOT PEPPER SAUCE
- **3** CUPS HALVED CHERRY TOMATOES

1 In small saucepan, place 2 inches water. Bring to a boil over medium-high heat. Add carrots; cook until blanched, about 2 minutes. Drain. Rinse under cold water; drain.

2 In medium serving bowl, combine carrots, chicken, cabbage and all but 3 tablespoons cilantro.

3 To make dressing, in small bowl, combine lime juice, oil, garlic, cayenne and salt until well mixed. Add hot pepper sauce to taste.

4 Pour dressing over chicken-vegetable mixture; toss gently to evenly coat. Top with cherry tomatoes and remaining 3 tablespoons cilantro.

PREPARATION TIP

Other vegetables can be substituted or added to this colorful salad including jicama, red or green peppers, green beans, etc.

Calories: 593 · Protein: 54 g
Fat: 35 g/53% calories from fat · Carbohydrate: 14 g
Cholesterol: 143 mg · Sodium: 430 mg

Oriental Chicken Salad

Serves 6

- **4** SKINLESS, BONELESS CHICKEN BREAST HALVES (ABOUT 1¼ POUNDS)
- **2** CUPS CHICKEN BROTH
- **6** SLICES ¼-INCH-THICK FRESH GINGER
- **¼** TEASPOON RED PEPPER FLAKES
- **1** CUP LONG-GRAIN RICE
- **2** CLOVES GARLIC, MINCED
- **6** TABLESPOONS ORIENTAL SESAME OIL
- **¼** CUP ORANGE JUICE
- **3** TABLESPOONS RICE WINE OR CIDER VINEGAR
- **2** TABLESPOONS REDUCED-SODIUM SOY SAUCE
- **¼** TEASPOON PEPPER
- **3** MEDIUM CARROTS, THINLY SLICED ON DIAGONAL
- **8** OUNCES MUSHROOMS, SLICED
- **8** OUNCES FRESH OR FROZEN SNOW PEAS, SLICED LENGTHWISE INTO SLIVERS
- **4** GREEN ONIONS, FINELY CHOPPED

1 Preheat broiler. Place chicken on broiler pan.

2 In medium saucepan, combine chicken broth, ½ ginger and red pepper flakes. Bring to a boil over medium-high heat. Add rice. Reduce heat to medium-low; cover and simmer until rice is tender, about 20 minutes. Uncover and set aside.

3 Meanwhile, in small bowl, combine remaining ginger with garlic and 1 tablespoon sesame oil.

4 Brush chicken with ½ ginger-garlic mixture. Broil chicken 4 inches from heat source until lightly browned, about 6 minutes. Turn; brush with remaining ginger-garlic mixture. Broil until chicken is cooked through, about 7 minutes. Remove and cool slightly; cut across the grain into ¼-inch-thick slices.

5 In large salad bowl, combine remaining 5 tablespoons oil, orange juice, vinegar, soy sauce and pepper. Add rice, chicken, carrots, mushrooms, snow peas and scallions; toss gently to evenly coat.

Calories: 389 · Protein: 27 g
Fat: 16 g/37% calories from fat · Carbohydrate: 34 g
Cholesterol: 55 mg · Sodium: 608 mg

Minted Chicken Salad

A takeoff on combinations commonly found in Greek cooking, this delicious salad includes the tang of a lemon dressing, the freshness of mint and the saltiness of feta cheese.

Serves 4

1 POUND SMALL RED POTATOES, HALVED
8 OUNCES FRESH GREEN BEANS, CUT INTO 2-INCH PIECES
1 CUP REDUCED-SODIUM CHICKEN BROTH, FAT REMOVED
2 SKINLESS, BONELESS CHICKEN BREAST HALVES (ABOUT ¾ POUND)
¾ CUP BUTTERMILK
2 TABLESPOONS FRESH LEMON JUICE
1 TABLESPOON HONEY
¼ TEASPOON SALT
¼ TEASPOON CAYENNE PEPPER
⅓ CUP CHOPPED FRESH MINT
12 OUNCES PACKED FRESH SPINACH LEAVES, WASHED AND TORN (8 CUPS)
2 CUPS CHERRY TOMATOES, HALVED
1 CUP CRUMBLED FETA CHEESE

PREPARATION TIP

If the saltiness of the feta is objectionable or you're watching your sodium intake, rinse the cheese under cool water and drain it well before crumbling it. This washes away the salty brine the cheese is packed in.

1 In medium saucepan, place potatoes and enough water to cover over high heat. Bring to a boil; cook, partially covered, just until barely tender, about 10 to 15 minutes. Add green beans during last 2 minutes. Drain.

2 Meanwhile, in medium skillet, combine broth and chicken over medium heat. Bring to a boil. Reduce heat to low; simmer, uncovered, until chicken is cooked through, about 5 to 8 minutes. Remove chicken (reserving broth for another use) and cool slightly; cut across the grain into ½-inch-thick slices. Set aside.

3 To make dressing, in large bowl, combine buttermilk, lemon juice, honey, salt and cayenne until well mixed. Add mint; stir until well mixed. Add potatoes, green beans, chicken, spinach and tomatoes; toss gently to evenly coat.

4 Top with feta cheese.

Calories: 362 · Protein: 35 g
Fat: 8 g/19% calories from fat · Carbohydrate: 43 g
Cholesterol: 71 mg · Sodium: 680 mg

Lemon-Herb Chicken and Tomatoes

Serves 4

4 SKINLESS, BONELESS CHICKEN BREAST HALVES (ABOUT 1¼ POUNDS)
2 CLOVES GARLIC, PEELED
⅓ CUP FRESH LEAVES OR 2 TEASPOONS DRIED BASIL
1½ TEASPOONS FRESH LEAVES OR ½ TEASPOON DRIED THYME
¼ CUP OLIVE OR OTHER VEGETABLE OIL
¼ CUP LEMON JUICE
2 TEASPOONS GRATED LEMON PEEL (OPTIONAL)
3 MEDIUM PLUM OR BEEFSTEAK TOMATOES, SLICED

1 Preheat broiler. Place chicken on broiler pan; set aside.

2 To make dressing, in food processor or blender, mince garlic. Add basil and thyme; process 10 seconds. Add oil, lemon juice and lemon peel, if desired; process until blended. Measure out 3 tablespoons dressing for basting chicken.

3 Brush chicken with 1 tablespoon dressing. Broil 4 inches from heat source until lightly browned, about 7 to 10 minutes.

4 Place tomatoes in shallow bowl. Add remaining dressing; toss gently to coat and set aside.

5 Turn chicken; brush with remaining 2 tablespoons dressing. Broil until lightly browned and chicken is cooked through, about 6 minutes. Slice the chicken on the diagonal across the grain. Serve tomatoes and chicken with excess dressing.

Calories: 289 · Protein: 33 g
Fat: 15 g/46% calories from fat · Carbohydrate: 3 g
Cholesterol: 82 mg · Sodium: 98 mg

Pasta Primavera Salad

Serves 6

½ CUP PACKED FRESH BASIL, FINELY CHOPPED OR 2 TEASPOONS DRIED BASIL
3 TABLESPOONS OLIVE OR OTHER VEGETABLE OIL
2 TABLESPOONS LEMON JUICE
1 TABLESPOON DIJON MUSTARD
2 TEASPOONS GRATED LEMON PEEL
½ TEASPOON SALT
¼ TEASPOON RED PEPPER FLAKES
¼ TEASPOON PEPPER
3 CLOVES GARLIC, PEELED
8 OUNCES EGG NOODLES
1 PACKAGE (10 OUNCES) FROZEN PEAS
1 PACKAGE (10 OUNCES) FROZEN ASPARAGUS
1 POUND COOKED CHICKEN BREASTS, CUT INTO THIN STRIPS
2 TABLESPOONS GRATED PARMESAN CHEESE

1 In large saucepan or Dutch oven, place enough water to cook noodles. Bring to a boil over medium-high heat.

2 In large salad bowl, to make dressing, combine basil, oil, lemon juice, mustard, lemon peel, salt, red pepper flakes and pepper until well mixed; set aside.

3 Add garlic and noodles to boiling water; cook until noodles are al dente, about 8 to 10 minutes.

4 Meanwhile, place frozen peas and asparagus in colander. Pour cooked noodles and water into colander over vegetables; drain. Rinse under cool water; drain. Cut asparagus into ¾-inch pieces.

5 Mash garlic with fork; add to dressing. Add noodles, vegetables, chicken and Parmesan cheese; toss gently to evenly coat.

Calories: 388 · Protein: 32 g
Fat: 12 g/29% calories from fat · Carbohydrate: 35 g
Cholesterol: 98 mg · Sodium: 346 mg

French Potato-Chicken Salad

For potatoes that hold their shape well and make a more attractive presentation, choose a waxy boiling potato, such as the round "Red Bliss" or the tapered tan "White Rose."

Serves 6

1 POUND BOILING POTATOES, UNPEELED, CUT INTO ½-INCH CHUNKS
8 OUNCES FRESH GREEN BEANS, CUT INTO 2-INCH PIECES
2 SKINLESS, BONELESS CHICKEN BREAST HALVES (ABOUT ¾ POUND), CUT INTO BITE-SIZE PIECES
¼ CUP OLIVE OR OTHER VEGETABLE OIL
2 TABLESPOONS WHITE WINE OR CIDER VINEGAR
1 TABLESPOON DIJON MUSTARD
¾ TEASPOON WORCESTERSHIRE SAUCE
2 TABLESPOONS MINCED FRESH OR 2 TEASPOONS DRIED DILL
¼ TEASPOON SALT
PEPPER TO TASTE

1 Place potatoes in steamer basket over boiling water over medium heat. Reduce heat to medium-low and steam 10 minutes. Add beans; cover and cook until potatoes are tender and beans are crisp-tender, about 5 to 8 minutes. Transfer to serving bowl; set aside.

2 Place chicken in steamer basket; cover and cook until opaque and cooked through, about 6 to 8 minutes. Transfer to serving bowl with vegetables.

3 To make dressing, in small bowl, combine oil, vinegar, mustard, Worcestershire sauce, dill, salt and pepper.

4 Add dressing to chicken-vegetable mixture; toss gently to evenly coat. Serve warm or at room temperature.

Calories: 199 · Protein: 11 g
Fat: 10 g/45% calories from fat · Carbohydrate: 17 g
Cholesterol: 22 mg · Sodium: 205 mg

Chicken Niçoise-Style

Serves 4

- ¾ POUND SMALL NEW POTATOES, CUT INTO 2-INCH WEDGES
- ½ POUND FRESH GREEN BEANS, CUT INTO 2-INCH PIECES
- **1** TABLESPOON CANOLA OR OTHER VEGETABLE OIL
- **2** SMALL SKINLESS, BONELESS CHICKEN BREAST HALVES (ABOUT ¾ POUND)
- ¼ CUP EXTRA-VIRGIN OLIVE OIL
- ⅓ CUP WHITE WINE
- **1** TEASPOON LEMON JUICE
- ¼ TEASPOON DIJON MUSTARD
- **1** CLOVE GARLIC, MINCED
- ¼ TEASPOON CHOPPED FRESH BASIL
- SALT AND PEPPER TO TASTE
- **8** OUNCES CHERRY TOMATOES, HALVED
- **2** OUNCES PITTED KALAMATA OLIVES, CUT INTO LENGTHWISE QUARTERS
- **16** ROMAINE OR OTHER SALAD GREENS, TORN INTO BITE-SIZE PIECES

1 In medium saucepan, combine potatoes and boiling water to cover. Bring to a boil and cook 2 minutes. Add green beans; cover and cook until potatoes are tender, about 5 minutes. Drain. Rinse under cool water; drain. Set aside.

2 In small skillet, heat oil over medium-high heat until warm. Add chicken; cook, stirring occasionally, until cooked through, about 4 to 6 minutes.

3 In large salad bowl, to make dressing, combine oil, wine, lemon juice, mustard, garlic, basil, salt and pepper to taste. Add potatoes, green beans, chicken, cherry tomatoes and olives; toss gently to evenly coat. Serve on bed of greens.

Calories: 395 · Protein: 23 g
Fat: 22 g/51% calories from fat · Carbohydrate: 24 g
Cholesterol: 53 mg · Sodium: 414 mg

Chicken Cobb Salad

Serves 4

- **2** SMALL SKINLESS, BONELESS CHICKEN BREAST HALVES (ABOUT ¾ POUND)
- ⅔ CUP PLAIN NONFAT YOGURT
- **3** TABLESPOONS MANGO CHUTNEY
- **2** TABLESPOONS REDUCED-FAT MAYONNAISE
- **1** TABLESPOON FRESH LEMON JUICE
- ½ TEASPOON SALT
- **2** MEDIUM TART APPLES, CORED AND DICED
- **1** RIB CELERY, FINELY CHOPPED
- **2** TABLESPOONS MINCED GREEN ONION
- **12** BOSTON LETTUCE LEAVES
- **1** OUNCE BLUE CHEESE, CRUMBLED

1 Preheat broiler. Place chicken on broiler pan. Broil 4 inches from heat source until cooked through, turning once, about 8 to 10 minutes. Remove and cool slightly; cut into ¾-inch chunks.

2 In large serving bowl, to make dressing, combine yogurt, chutney, mayonnaise, lemon juice and salt until well mixed. Add chicken, apples, celery and green onion; toss gently to evenly coat.

3 To serve, arrange salad on lettuce topped with blue cheese.

PREPARATION TIP
To cut down on cooking time, buy a ¾-inch-thick slice of cooked chicken or turkey from the deli department and cut into cubes.

Calories: 268 · Protein: 30 g
Fat: 6 g/20% calories from fat · Carbohydrate: 22 g
Cholesterol: 74 mg · Sodium: 654 mg

Chinese Sesame-Ginger Chicken Salad

The light flavorful sesame-ginger dressing and chicken can be teamed up with many other vegetables, such as cooked asparagus, broccoli florets, snow peas or green beans, for all kinds of chicken salad variations.

Serves 4

- **2** SKINLESS, BONELESS CHICKEN BREAST HALVES (ABOUT ¾ POUND)
- **⅓** CUP RICE WINE OR OTHER MILD VINEGAR
- **¼** CUP CHICKEN BROTH, FAT REMOVED
- **2** SLICES ¼-INCH-THICK FRESH GINGER, PEELED, MINCED
- **1** TABLESPOON ORIENTAL SESAME OIL
- **1** TABLESPOON DIJON MUSTARD
- **2** CLOVES GARLIC, MINCED
- **1** TEASPOON SOY SAUCE
- **3** GREEN ONIONS, COARSELY CHOPPED
- **1** LARGE RED PEPPER, CUT INTO BITE-SIZE PIECES
- **2** MEDIUM CARROTS, CUT INTO ¼-INCH COINS
- **1** CAN (8 OUNCES) SLICED BAMBOO SHOOTS, DRAINED
- **8** RED LEAF OR ROMAINE LETTUCE LEAVES, TORN

1 Place chicken in steamer basket over boiling water over medium heat. Reduce heat to medium-low and steam until chicken is done, about 5 to 8 minutes. Remove and cool slightly; cut across the grain into ¼-inch-thick slices. Set aside.

2 To make dressing, in small bowl, combine vinegar, chicken broth, ginger, sesame oil, mustard, garlic and soy sauce until well mixed.

3 In medium skillet, heat half the dressing until warm. Add green onions and cook until wilted, about 1 minute.

4 Add reserved chicken, red pepper, carrots, and bamboo shoots; cook, stirring, until just heated through, about 3 minutes.

5 In large serving bowl, combine chicken-vegetable mixture, lettuce and remaining dressing; toss gently to evenly coat.

PREPARATION TIP

Chicken broth prepared from instant bouillon powder or cubes can be used in place of canned chicken broth. When using canned, be sure to skim off the fat floating on top.

Calories: 170 · Protein: 22 g
Fat: 5 g/26% calories from fat · Carbohydrate: 9 g
Cholesterol: 49 mg · Sodium: 301 mg

Warm Sautéed Vegetables and Pasta Salad

Serves 4

- **8** OUNCES SMALL PASTA (SMALL SHELLS, ORZO, ETC.)
- **2** TABLESPOONS VEGETABLE OIL
- **3** CLOVES GARLIC, MINCED
- **1** MEDIUM RED ONION, COARSELY CHOPPED
- **1** LARGE CARROT, COARSELY CHOPPED
- **1** MEDIUM ZUCCHINI, COARSELY CHOPPED
- **8** OUNCES COOKED CHICKEN, CUT INTO ½-INCH PIECES
- **3** TABLESPOONS LEMON JUICE
- **2** TABLESPOONS DIJON MUSTARD
- **1** TEASPOON DRIED OREGANO
- **½** TEASPOON SALT
- **½** TEASPOON PEPPER
- **⅓** CUP GRATED PARMESAN CHEESE

1 In large saucepan or Dutch oven, place enough water to cook pasta. Bring to a boil over medium-high heat.

2 Add pasta to boiling water; cook until pasta is al dente, about 8 to 10 minutes.

3 Meanwhile, in large skillet, heat 1 tablespoon oil over medium-high heat until warm. Add garlic and onion; cook until onion begins to brown, about 5 minutes.

4 Add remaining oil to skillet; add carrot and zucchini; cook until carrot is just tender, about 5 minutes. Remove from heat.

5 Drain pasta; place in large serving bowl. Add cooked vegetable mixture and chicken.

6 To make dressing, combine lemon juice, mustard, oregano, salt and pepper. Add to pasta-vegetable-chicken mixture with Parmesan cheese; toss gently to evenly coat.

Calories: 443 · Protein: 28 g
Fat: 13 g/26% calories from fat · Carbohydrate: 51 g
Cholesterol: 50 mg · Sodium: 708 mg

Chinese Chicken Salad with Peanuts

Serves 4

- **2** LARGE SKINLESS, BONELESS CHICKEN BREAST HALVES (ABOUT 1 POUND)
- **⅓** CUP HOISIN SAUCE
- **¼** CUP APPLE JUICE
- **1** TEASPOON VEGETABLE OIL
- **¼** TEASPOON SALT
- **2** RED PEPPERS, CUT INTO THIN STRIPS
- **2** CARROTS, SHREDDED
- **2** CUPS BEAN SPROUTS
- **1** CAN (8 OUNCES) SLICED WATER CHESTNUTS, RINSED AND DRAINED
- **2** TABLESPOONS FINELY CHOPPED GREEN ONION
- **½** TEASPOON GROUND GINGER
- **3** CUPS ¼-INCH-WIDE SHREDDED ROMAINE LETTUCE
- **1** TABLESPOON COARSELY CHOPPED UNSALTED DRY-ROASTED PEANUTS

1 Preheat broiler. Place chicken on broiler rack; set aside.

2 In large bowl, to make dressing, combine hoisin sauce, apple juice, oil and salt. Measure out 2 tablespoons dressing for basting chicken. Set remaining aside.

3 Brush chicken with 1 tablespoon dressing. Broil 4 inches from heat source until browned. Turn, brush with remaining tablespoon dressing. Broil until cooked through, about 8 to 10 minutes. Remove and cool slightly; cut across the grain into ¼-inch-thick slices.

4 To bowl with reserved dressing add chicken, peppers, carrots, sprouts, water chestnuts, green onion and ginger; toss gently to evenly coat.

5 Serve over lettuce topped with peanuts.

Calories: 275 · Protein: 31 g
Fat: 4 g/13% calories from fat · Carbohydrate: 29 g
Cholesterol: 66 mg · Sodium: 914 mg

New Delhi Chicken Salad

Serves 4

- **2** LARGE SKINLESS, BONELESS CHICKEN BREAST HALVES (ABOUT 1 POUND)
- **½** TEASPOON DRIED THYME
- **½** TEASPOON SALT
- **½** CUP PLAIN NONFAT YOGURT
- **2** TABLESPOONS KETCHUP
- **1** TABLESPOON MAYONNAISE
- **2** TEASPOONS DIJON MUSTARD
- **⅛** TEASPOON PEPPER
- **2** RIBS CELERY, DICED
- **1** RED ONION, MINCED
- **1** CUCUMBER, HALVED LENGTHWISE, SEEDED AND DICED
- **¼** CUP DICED SWEET GHERKINS
- **3** TABLESPOONS CHOPPED BLACK OLIVES
- **12** ROMAINE LETTUCE LEAVES
- **2** TOMATOES, EACH CUT INTO 8 WEDGES

1 Preheat broiler. Rub chicken with mixture of thyme and salt. Place chicken on broiler pan. Broil 4 inches from heat source until browned. Turn; broil until cooked through, about 8 to 10 minutes. Remove and cool slightly; shred and set aside.

2 In medium bowl, to make dressing, combine yogurt, ketchup, mayonnaise, mustard and pepper. Add chicken, celery, onion, cucumber, gherkins and olives; toss gently to evenly coat.

3 Serve on lettuce leaves topped with chicken-vegetable mixture with tomatoes on the side.

Calories: 219 · Protein: 23 g
Fat: 6 g/27% calories from fat · Carbohydrate: 16 g
Cholesterol: 56 mg · Sodium: 602 mg

Thai Chicken, Shrimp and Fruit Salad

Serves 4

- **1** SMALL CLOVE GARLIC, MINCED
- **¼** CUP FRESH MINCED OR 1 TEASPOON DRIED MINT
- **⅓** CUP LIME JUICE (ABOUT 2 LIMES)
- **¼** CUP ORIENTAL SESAME OIL
- **3** TABLESPOONS HONEY
- **2** TEASPOONS GRATED LIME PEEL
- **¼** TEASPOON RED PEPPER FLAKES
- SALT TO TASTE
- **8** OUNCES COOKED CHICKEN, CUT INTO ½-INCH CUBES
- **8** OUNCES COOKED, DEVEINED BABY SHRIMP
- **1** MEDIUM ORANGE, PEELED, CUT CROSSWISE INTO ¼-INCH HALF-ROUNDS
- **2** CUPS FRESH OR DRAINED CANNED PINEAPPLE CHUNKS
- **2** CUPS SEEDLESS RED GRAPES
- **½** CUP UNSALTED PEANUTS (OPTIONAL)

1 In large serving bowl, to make dressing, combine garlic, mint, lime juice, oil, honey, lime peel, red pepper flakes and salt until well mixed.

2 Add chicken, shrimp, orange, pineapple and grapes; toss gently to evenly coat. Serve topped with peanuts, if desired.

PREPARATION TIP
This salad can be made in advance; however, if using fresh pineapple do not add until just before serving.

Calories: 411 · Protein: 30 g
Fat: 17 g/37% calories from fat · Carbohydrate: 37 g
Cholesterol: 154 mg · Sodium: 205 mg

Roast Chicken with Pecan-Rice Dressing

Cooking the chicken breast-side down for the first thirty minutes, then turning, makes this bird extra moist and tender. Placing the seasoning under the skin adds extra flavor.

Serves 4

3 SHALLOTS OR GREEN ONIONS, MINCED
¼ CUP CHOPPED FRESH BASIL
3 CLOVES GARLIC, MINCED
1 TEASPOON OLIVE OR OTHER VEGETABLE OIL
¾ TEASPOON SALT
¼ TEASPOON DRIED SAGE
1 WHOLE CHICKEN (3½ POUNDS)
2 TABLESPOONS FRESH LEMON JUICE
1 LARGE ONION, DICED
1 MEDIUM CARROT, FINELY CHOPPED
2 CUPS WATER
2 CUPS THINLY SLICED MUSHROOMS
1 CUP LONG-GRAIN RICE
4 TEASPOONS CHOPPED PECANS
2 CUPS REDUCED-SODIUM CHICKEN BROTH, FAT REMOVED
¼ CUP ALL-PURPOSE FLOUR

1 Preheat oven to 375°. In small bowl, combine shallots, 2 tablespoons basil, ⅓ garlic, oil, ½ teaspoon salt and sage. Sprinkle chicken cavity with lemon juice. With fingers, carefully loosen skin from breast, leaving skin intact. Spread shallot-basil mixture under skin. Tie legs.

2 On rack in small roasting pan, place chicken breast-side down; bake 30 minutes. Turn breast-side up; bake, basting occasionally with pan juices, until chicken is cooked through, about 30 minutes.

3 Meanwhile, in medium oven- and flameproof 2-quart casserole, combine remaining garlic, onion, carrot and ¼ cup water over medium heat; cook 5 minutes. Add mushrooms; cook 5 minutes. Add remaining 2 tablespoons basil, 1¾ cups water and ¼ teaspoon salt, rice and pecans. Cover and bake with chicken during last 30 minutes until rice is tender.

4 Transfer chicken to serving platter; pour off any fat from pan. Place pan over medium-high heat; add broth. Bring to a boil, stirring to loosen browned bits. Stir in flour until smooth; cook, stirring constantly, until thickened, about 3 to 5 minutes. Serve chicken sliced with rice dressing and gravy.

PREPARATION TIP

If desired, the rice dressing can be cooked on the stovetop. Bring 2 cups water, vegetables, herbs, salt and pepper to a boil. Add rice. Reduce heat to low; cover and simmer until rice is tender, about 15 to 20 minutes.

Calories: 550 · Protein: 50 g
Fat: 14 g/23 calories from fat · Carbohydrate: 54 g
Cholesterol: 127 mg · Sodium: 866 mg

Chicken Breasts with Red Pepper Purée

Add extra richness to the pepper purée by adding two tablespoons sour cream to the purée just before serving. For the richness without extra fat use nonfat sour cream.

Serves 4

- **2** TABLESPOONS LEMON JUICE
- **1** TABLESPOON OLIVE OR OTHER VEGETABLE OIL
- **1** TEASPOON DRIED THYME
- **¼** TEASPOON PEPPER
- **4** SKINLESS, BONELESS CHICKEN BREAST HALVES (ABOUT 1¼ POUNDS)
- **2** TABLESPOONS BUTTER OR MARGARINE
- **1** MEDIUM ONION, COARSELY CHOPPED
- **2** CLOVES GARLIC, MINCED
- **1** LARGE RED PEPPER, CUT INTO BITE-SIZE PIECES
- **2** TEASPOONS TOMATO PASTE
- **1½** TEASPOONS GRATED LEMON PEEL (OPTIONAL)
- **¼** TEASPOON SALT

1 Preheat broiler.

2 In medium bowl, combine 1 tablespoon lemon juice, oil, ½ teaspoon thyme and pepper. Add chicken; turn to coat and set aside.

3 In small saucepan, melt butter over medium-high heat until warm. Add onion and garlic and cook until onion is tender, about 3 minutes. Add remaining 1 tablespoon lemon juice, remaining ½ teaspoon thyme, red pepper, tomato paste, lemon peel, if desired, and salt. Reduce heat to low; cover and simmer until pepper is softened, about 12 minutes.

4 Place chicken on broiler pan. Broil 4 inches from heat source until lightly browned, about 7 to 10 minutes. Turn; broil until golden brown, about 6 to 8 minutes.

5 To make purée, in food processor or blender, place cooked pepper mixture and process until smooth. Serve chicken on bed of red pepper purée.

PREPARATION TIP

To make the sauce in half the time, in medium microwave-safe bowl place all the ingredients in Step 3; cover and cook on High (100% power) until pepper is softened, about 6 minutes, stirring once. Continue as directed in Step 5 above.

Calories: 257 · Protein: 34 g
Fat: 11 g/38% calories from fat · Carbohydrate: 5 g
Cholesterol: 98 mg · Sodium: 311 mg

Citrus-Marinated Chicken

Serves 4

2 LEMONS
1 ORANGE
¼ CUP MAPLE SYRUP
1 TABLESPOON OLIVE OIL
2 TEASPOONS DRIED THYME
½ TEASPOON PEPPER
2½ POUNDS CHICKEN WINGS AND DRUMSTICKS

1 Grate peel from lemons and orange and then squeeze juice. Set juice aside. In small bowl, combine grated lemon and orange peels and maple syrup; set aside.

2 In shallow bowl, combine reserved lemon and orange juices, oil, thyme and pepper. Add chicken; toss to evenly coat. Cover and refrigerate, turning occasionally, at least 4 hours or overnight.

3 Prepare broiler or grill according to manufacturer's directions. Broil or grill chicken 4 inches from heat source, turning once, until lightly browned, about 20 minutes. Brush with maple syrup mixture; broil or grill 1 minute. Turn; brush with maple syrup mixture; broil or grill 1 minute. Serve with remaining sauce, if desired.

PREPARATION TIP
Resealable heavy plastic bags are excellent for marinating; just toss or change position to 'turn.'

Calories: 475 · Protein: 50 g
Fat: 21 g/41% calories from fat · Carbohydrate: 18 g
Cholesterol: 171 mg · Sodium: 174 mg

Chicken Marsala

Serves 4

4 SKINLESS, BONELESS CHICKEN BREAST HALVES (ABOUT 1¼ POUNDS)
2 TABLESPOONS ALL-PURPOSE FLOUR
2 TABLESPOONS UNSALTED BUTTER OR MARGARINE
4 CUPS SLICED MUSHROOMS
1 CUP CHICKEN BROTH, FAT REMOVED
½ CUP MARSALA WINE
SALT AND PEPPER TO TASTE
1 TABLESPOON CHOPPED PARSLEY (OPTIONAL)

1 Between plastic wrap or wax paper pound chicken until ¼ inch thick. Coat chicken, evenly with flour.

2 In large skillet, heat butter over medium heat until hot and foaming. Add coated chicken cutlets; cook, turning, until browned, about 4 to 6 minutes. Remove and set aside.

3 To same skillet add mushrooms; cook until lightly browned. Reduce heat to low; cook until soft, about 2 to 3 minutes.

4 Add chicken broth and wine. Increase heat to high. Bring to a boil; cook, stirring occasionally, until thickened and reduced by half, about 5 minutes.

5 Return chicken to skillet. Reduce heat to low; simmer until chicken is cooked through, about 2 to 3 minutes.

6 Serve chicken topped with mushroom sauce and sprinkled with parsley, if desired.

Calories: 321 · Protein: 36 g
Fat: 11 g/31% calories from fat · Carbohydrate: 10 g
Cholesterol: 105 mg · Sodium: 330 mg

Chicken Cordon Bleu

Serves 4

- **4** SKINLESS, BONELESS CHICKEN BREAST HALVES (ABOUT 1¼ POUNDS)
- SALT AND PEPPER TO TASTE
- **4** THIN SLICES PROSCIUTTO OR HAM
- **4** THIN SLICES GRUYÈRE OR SWISS CHEESE
- **⅓** CUP ALL-PURPOSE FLOUR
- **1** LARGE EGG
- **⅔** CUP DRIED BREADCRUMBS
- **2** TABLESPOONS CHOPPED FRESH OR 2 TEASPOONS DRIED PARSLEY
- **2** TABLESPOONS BUTTER OR MARGARINE

1 Between plastic wrap or wax paper, pound chicken until ¼ inch thick. Season with salt and pepper. Layer 1 slice prosciutto then 1 slice cheese; roll up folding in sides. Secure with toothpicks.

2 Place flour on wax paper; in shallow bowl, beat egg with 1 tablespoon water and on wax paper place breadcrumbs mixed with parsley. Dip chicken rolls in flour, egg mixture then breadcrumbs to evenly and completely coat. Cover and refrigerate at least 1 hour up to 24 hours.

3 In large skillet, heat butter over medium heat until hot and foaming. Add coated chicken rolls; cook, turning, until browned and cooked through, about 12 minutes.

PREPARATION TIP
Be sure to totally fold in sides and secure tightly or the cheese will melt out into pan.

Calories: 524 · Protein: 52 g
Fat: 22 g/39% calories from fat · Carbohydrate: 25 g
Cholesterol: 215 mg · Sodium: 773 mg

Country Captain

Serves 4

- **½** CUP ALL-PURPOSE FLOUR
- **1** TEASPOON SALT
- **¼** TEASPOON PEPPER
- **2½** POUNDS CHICKEN PIECES
- **2** TABLESPOONS UNSALTED BUTTER OR MARGARINE
- **2** TABLESPOONS VEGETABLE OIL
- **1** MEDIUM ONION, CHOPPED
- **3** CLOVES GARLIC, LIGHTLY CRUSHED
- **2** TEASPOONS CURRY POWDER
- **½** TEASPOON DRIED THYME
- **2** CANS (16 OUNCES EACH) NO-SALT-ADDED TOMATOES, BROKEN UP
- **1** CUP RAISINS
- **¼** CUP CHOPPED PARSLEY
- **½** CUP SLICED ALMONDS, TOASTED

1 On wax paper, combine flour, ½ teaspoon salt and pepper. Coat chicken evenly with flour mixture. In large saucepan or Dutch oven, heat butter and oil over medium-high heat until hot. Add coated chicken; cook, turning, until browned, about 8 to 10 minutes. Remove and set aside.

2 Pour off all but 1 tablespoon fat. Add remaining ½ teaspoon salt, onion, garlic, curry powder and thyme. Reduce heat to low; cook, stirring to loosen any brown bits, 5 minutes.

3 Add undrained tomatoes and return chicken to saucepan. Cover and simmer until chicken is cooked through, about 20 minutes. Stir in raisins and parsley. Serve sprinkled with almonds.

Calories: 705 · Protein: 54 g
Fat: 39 g/49% calories from fat · Carbohydrate: 56 g
Cholesterol: 156 mg · Sodium: 730 mg

Spanish-Style Chicken

The century-old trick of thickening a sauce with bread is a Catalan technique that adds subtle flavor and body without fat.

Serves 4

- **1** JAR (4 OUNCES) ROASTED RED PEPPERS OR PIMIENTOS, RINSED AND DRAINED
- **2** CANS (4 OUNCES EACH) MILD GREEN CHILIES, RINSED AND DRAINED
- **2** SLICES FIRM WHITE SANDWICH BREAD, TOASTED, COARSELY TORN
- **¼** CUP CHICKEN BROTH, FAT REMOVED
- **¼** CUP DARK RAISINS
- **2** TABLESPOONS SLIVERED BLANCHED ALMONDS
- **½** TEASPOON SEEDED, CHOPPED PICKLED JALAPEÑO PEPPER
- **½** TEASPOON SALT
- **4** FLOUR TORTILLAS (6-INCH SIZE)
- **1** TABLESPOON ALL-PURPOSE FLOUR
- **¼** TEASPOON PEPPER
- **4** SKINLESS, BONELESS CHICKEN BREAST HALVES (ABOUT 1¼ POUNDS)
- **2** TEASPOONS VEGETABLE OIL
- **1** SMALL GREEN ONION, THINLY SLICED

1 Cut one red pepper half into thin strips; set aside. In food processor or blender, combine remaining red peppers, the chilies, bread, broth, 2 tablespoons raisins, 1 tablespoon almonds, the jalapeño pepper and ¼ teaspoon salt; process until smooth. Set aside.

2 Preheat oven to 350°. Wrap tortillas in foil; set aside.

3 In plastic or paper bag or shallow plate combine flour, remaining ¼ teaspoon salt and pepper. Add chicken; shake to coat chicken well. Remove chicken.

4 In large nonstick skillet, heat oil over medium heat until hot. Add chicken; cook, turning once, until golden, about 5 minutes.

5 Add reserved pepper sauce. Increase heat to medium-high. Bring to a boil. Reduce heat to low; cover and simmer until chicken is cooked through, about 8 minutes.

6 Meanwhile, place tortillas in oven; bake until heated through, about 5 minutes.

7 Remove chicken and cool slightly; cut across the grain into ½-inch-thick slices. Set aside.

8 To serve, on each heated tortilla place ¼ sliced chicken and sauce, ½ tablespoon raisins, ¼ remaining almonds, ¼ reserved red pepper strips and ¼ green onion.

PREPARATION TIP

To reduce the fat even more, the chicken can be broiled or grilled, sliced and then heated in the sauce.

Calories: 319 · Protein: 31 g
Fat: 8 g/1.2 g calories from fat · Carbohydrate: 30 g
Cholesterol: 66 mg · Sodium: 663 mg

Garlic Chicken

Serves 6

- **1** TABLESPOON BUTTER OR MARGARINE
- **1** TABLESPOON OLIVE OR OTHER VEGETABLE OIL
- **4** POUNDS CHICKEN PIECES
- **½** CUP CHICKEN BROTH, FAT REMOVED
- **½** CUP DRY WHITE WINE
- **40** CLOVES GARLIC, UNPEELED (3 LARGE HEADS)
- **1** TEASPOON DRIED OREGANO
- **1** TEASPOON DRIED THYME
- **¾** TEASPOON DRIED MARJORAM
- **½** TEASPOON PEPPER

1 Preheat oven to 375°.

2 In large skillet, heat butter and oil over medium-high heat until warm. Add half of the chicken; cook, turning, until golden brown, about 10 minutes. Transfer to large ovenproof casserole or deep baking dish. Repeat with remaining chicken.

3 Pour off all but 1 tablespoon fat. Add broth, wine, garlic, oregano, thyme, marjoram and pepper. Bring to a boil, stirring to loosen any brown bits. Pour broth-herb mixture over chicken. Cover tightly and bake until chicken is cooked through, about 45 to 60 minutes.

PREPARATION TIP

Soft-cooked garlic cloves make a delicious spread for bread. Just squeeze the unpeeled clove from the smaller end to squirt out the soft roasted garlic.

Calories: 442 · Protein: 56 g
Fat: 18 g/40% calories from fat · Carbohydrate: 6 g
Cholesterol: 174 mg · Sodium: 247 mg

Lemony Garlic Chicken

Serves 4

- **1** POUND SMALL RED POTATOES, CUT INTO QUARTERS
- **6** CLOVES GARLIC, 2 UNPEELED AND 4 PEELED
- **4** SPRIGS FRESH OR 1 TEASPOON DRIED THYME
- **2** SPRIGS FRESH OR ¾ TEASPOON DRIED ROSEMARY
- **¾** TEASPOON SALT
- **½** TEASPOON PEPPER
- **1** TEASPOON OLIVE OIL
- **1** WHOLE CHICKEN (3½ POUNDS)
- **1** BAY LEAF
- **2** LEMONS, 1 PIERCED SEVERAL TIMES WITH A FORK, 1 THINLY SLICED

1 Preheat oven to 375°. In medium baking pan, combine potatoes, unpeeled garlic, 2 sprigs thyme, 1 sprig rosemary, ¼ teaspoon salt and ¼ teaspoon pepper. Drizzle potatoes with oil; set aside.

2 Sprinkle chicken cavity with remaining ½ teaspoon salt and remaining ¼ teaspoon pepper. Place bay leaf, peeled garlic and pierced lemon in cavity.

3 With fingers, carefully loosen skin from breast, leaving skin intact. Tuck remaining thyme, rosemary and lemon slices under the skin. Tie legs.

4 In small roasting pan on rack, place chicken breast-side down.

5 Bake chicken and potatoes 30 minutes. Turn chicken; cook, basting chicken with pan juices and stirring potatoes, until chicken is tender and potatoes are cooked, about 30 minutes.

Calories: 392 · Protein: 44 g
Fat: 12 g/28 calories from fat · Carbohydrate: 28 g
Cholesterol: 127 mg · Sodium: 546 mg

Chicken Stroganoff

This variation on the classic Beef Stroganoff uses chicken, mushrooms and plain yogurt to cut calories and still keep the rich flavor.

Serves 4

- **⅓** CUP ALL-PURPOSE FLOUR
- **½** TEASPOON SALT
- **¼** TEASPOON PEPPER
- **4** SKINLESS, BONELESS CHICKEN BREAST HALVES (ABOUT 1¼ POUNDS), CUT INTO BITE-SIZE PIECES
- **4** TABLESPOONS BUTTER OR MARGARINE
- **2** TABLESPOONS VEGETABLE OIL
- **1** MEDIUM ONION, CUT INTO WEDGES
- **½** POUND SMALL MUSHROOMS, HALVED
- **1** TABLESPOON DIJON MUSTARD
- **1** TABLESPOON PAPRIKA
- **½** CUP CHICKEN BROTH
- **¼** CUP SOUR CREAM, AT ROOM TEMPERATURE
- **¼** CUP PLAIN YOGURT, AT ROOM TEMPERATURE
- **8** OUNCES EGG NOODLES, COOKED, HOT

1 In plastic or paper bag, combine flour, salt and pepper. Add chicken pieces; shake to coat chicken well. Remove chicken and reserve excess flour mixture.

2 In large nonstick skillet, warm 1 tablespoon butter and 1 tablespoon oil over medium heat until butter is melted. Add onion and mushrooms; cook until onion is tender, about 4 minutes. Remove onion and mushrooms; set aside.

3 To same skillet add remaining oil; increase heat to medium-high. Add chicken; cook, turning occasionally, until light golden but not cooked through, about 3 minutes. Remove and keep warm.

4 To same skillet add remaining butter; warm until butter is melted. Stir in excess flour mixture. Cook until blended, about 1 minute.

5 Stir in mustard and paprika then chicken broth. Reduce heat to medium-low; add reserved onion, mushrooms and chicken. Cover and simmer 5 minutes. Stir in sour cream and yogurt; cook until heated through, about 2 minutes.

6 Serve chicken-onion mixture over hot noodles.

PREPARATION TIP

To save calories, decrease butter by 1 to 2 tablespoons and use plain nonfat yogurt and sour cream. Be sure the sauce doesn't boil after adding the dairy products or it may curdle.

Calories: 645 · Protein: 45 g
Fat: 27 g/37% calories from fat · Carbohydrate: 56 g
Cholesterol: 174 mg · Sodium: 751 mg

Chicken Pot Pie

Serves 4

1 CUP CHICKEN BROTH, FAT REMOVED
3 CARROTS, CUT INTO ½-INCH PIECES
1 LARGE ALL-PURPOSE POTATO, CUT INTO ½-INCH CHUNKS
1 PARSNIP, CUT INTO ½-INCH CHUNKS
½ TEASPOON SALT
1 CUP FROZEN PEARL ONIONS
1 CUP FROZEN PEAS
1 POUND SKINLESS, BONELESS CHICKEN THIGHS, CUT INTO 2-INCH PIECES
½ CUP EVAPORATED SKIM MILK
¼ CUP ALL-PURPOSE FLOUR
½ TEASPOON DRIED SAGE
¼ TEASPOON PEPPER
2 9-INCH PIE CRUSTS

1 Preheat oven to 425°. In large saucepan, combine broth, carrots, potato, parsnip and ¼ teaspoon salt over high heat. Bring to a boil. Reduce heat to low; cover and simmer until potato is almost tender, about 5 minutes. Stir in pearl onions, peas and chicken. Increase heat to high. Bring back to a boil. Reduce heat to low; cover and simmer until chicken is cooked through, about 5 minutes.

2 Meanwhile, in small saucepan, combine remaining ¼ teaspoon salt, evaporated milk, flour, sage and pepper over medium-high heat. Bring to a boil. Reduce heat to low; simmer, stirring occasionally, until sauce is as thick as heavy cream, about 2 minutes. Stir in chicken-vegetable mixture.

3 In 9-inch deep-dish pie plate, place ½ pastry; fill with chicken mixture. Spread mixture and top with remaining pastry; crimp edges to seal and cut slits on top. Bake 15 minutes. Reduce oven temperature to 325°. Bake until crust is brown, about 10 to 15 minutes.

Calories: 883 · Protein: 38 g
Fat: 34 g/35% calories from fat · Carbohydrate: 80 g
Cholesterol: 77 mg · Sodium: 1,190 mg

Chicken Dijonnaise

Serves 4

3 TABLESPOONS DIJON MUSTARD
2 TABLESPOONS HONEY
4 TEASPOONS CIDER VINEGAR
½ CUP FINELY CHOPPED CUCUMBER
½ CUP FINELY CHOPPED RED PEPPER
½ CUP FINELY CHOPPED TOMATO
3 TABLESPOONS FINELY CHOPPED GREEN ONION
⅛ TEASPOON PEPPER
4 SKINLESS, BONELESS CHICKEN BREAST HALVES (ABOUT 1¼ POUNDS)

1 Preheat broiler or grill according to manufacturer's directions. In 1-cup measure, combine mustard, honey and vinegar until well mixed. Place ¼ cup mustard-honey mixture in medium bowl and reserve remaining mixture.

2 To bowl add cucumber, red pepper, tomato, green onion and pepper; toss to evenly coat and set aside.

3 Brush chicken with reserved mustard-honey mixture. Broil or grill 4 inches from heat source until chicken is browned, about 4 minutes. Turn; broil or grill until chicken is cooked through, about 4 to 6 minutes. Serve chicken topped with vegetable mixture.

PREPARATION TIP
Grill double the amount of chicken at the same time and serve the grilled chicken cold over greens or on a hero roll with lettuce and tomato for a fast dinner.

Calories: 235 · Protein: 34 g
Fat: 5 g/21% calories from fat · Carbohydrate: 12 g
Cholesterol: 89 mg · Sodium: 231 mg

Chicken Paprika

This Hungarian favorite, which blends paprika and sour cream, needs gentle heat after the sour cream is added to prevent a curdled appearance.

Serves 4

- **2** TABLESPOONS ALL-PURPOSE FLOUR
- **2** TABLESPOONS PAPRIKA
- **¾** TEASPOON SALT
- **¼** TEASPOON PEPPER
- **2** TABLESPOONS OLIVE OR OTHER VEGETABLE OIL
- **2** TABLESPOONS UNSALTED BUTTER OR MARGARINE
- **4** GREEN ONIONS, COARSELY CHOPPED
- **3** CLOVES GARLIC, MINCED
- **4** SKINLESS, BONELESS CHICKEN BREAST HALVES (ABOUT 1¼ POUNDS), CUT ACROSS GRAIN INTO ¼-INCH THICK STRIPS
- **8** OUNCES SMALL MUSHROOMS, HALVED
- **½** CUP SOUR CREAM
- **¼** CUP PLAIN LOW-FAT YOGURT
- **1** CUP COARSELY CHOPPED CANNED WHOLE TOMATOES
- **½** CUP CHICKEN BROTH, FAT REMOVED
- **8** OUNCES WIDE EGG NOODLES, COOKED

1 In plastic or paper bag, combine flour, paprika, salt and pepper until well mixed; set aside.

2 In large skillet, heat 1 tablespoon oil and 1 tablespoon butter over medium-high heat until butter is melted. Add green onions and garlic; cook, stirring frequently, until green onions are tender, about 3 minutes.

3 Place chicken in flour-paprika mixture; toss until well coated. Reserve excess.

4 In same skillet, add coated chicken; cook, stirring frequently, until cooked through, about 5 minutes. Remove chicken and keep warm.

5 To same skillet add remaining oil and butter. Add mushrooms; cook, stirring occasionally, until wilted, about 5 minutes.

6 In small bowl, combine reserved flour mixture, sour cream and yogurt.

7 To skillet add tomatoes. Reduce heat to medium; add reserved chicken, broth and sour cream mixture. Cook, stirring occasionally, until heated through, about 2 minutes.

8 Serve chicken mixture over hot noodles.

PREPARATION TIP

Look in the poultry section of your supermarket for ready-to-use chicken strips to save preparation time.

Calories: 616 · Protein: 44 g
Fat: 26 g/39% calories from fat · Carbohydrate: 49 g
Cholesterol: 169 mg · Sodium: 624 mg

Southern-Fried Chicken Strips

Serves 4

- **⅓** CUP ALL-PURPOSE FLOUR
- **2** TABLESPOONS CHOPPED PARSLEY (OPTIONAL)
- **1** TEASPOON PAPRIKA
- **½** TEASPOON SALT
- **¼** TEASPOON PEPPER
- PINCH OF CAYENNE PEPPER
- **4** SKINLESS, BONELESS CHICKEN BREAST HALVES (ABOUT 1¼ POUNDS), CUT ACROSS THE GRAIN INTO ½-INCH-WIDE STRIPS
- **2** TABLESPOONS PLUS 1 TEASPOON OIL
- **¼** CUP DIJON OR WHOLE-GRAIN MUSTARD
- **1½** TEASPOONS HONEY
- **1** TEASPOON CIDER VINEGAR

1 In plastic or paper bag, combine flour, parsley, if desired, paprika, salt, pepper and cayenne. Add chicken strips; shake to coat chicken well.

2 In large nonstick skillet, heat 2 tablespoons oil over medium-high heat until hot. Add coated chicken strips in single layer; cook, turning frequently, until cooked through and golden, about 7 minutes. Drain on paper towels.

3 In small bowl, combine remaining 1 teaspoon oil, mustard, honey and vinegar until well mixed.

4 Serve chicken strips with honey-mustard mixture.

PREPARATION TIP

To soften crystallized or hard to pour honey, place jar without the cap in the microwave on High (100% power) for 30 to 45 seconds.

Calories: 292 · Protein: 34 g
Fat: 11 g/33% calories from fat · Carbohydrate: 13 g
Cholesterol: 82 mg · Sodium: 816 mg

Chicken, Carrot and Potato Stew

Serves 4

- **2** TABLESPOONS ALL-PURPOSE FLOUR
- **¾** TEASPOON SALT
- **¼** TEASPOON PEPPER
- **8** CHICKEN DRUMSTICKS, SKINNED (ABOUT 2 POUNDS)
- **1** TABLESPOON VEGETABLE OIL
- **3** CLOVES GARLIC, PEELED
- **4** MEDIUM CARROTS, THINLY SLICED
- **12** GREEN ONIONS, CUT INTO 2-INCH PIECES
- **1½** POUNDS SMALL RED POTATOES, THINLY SLICED
- **1½** TEASPOONS DRIED ROSEMARY
- **1** CUP DRY WHITE WINE
- **2** CUPS CHICKEN BROTH, FAT REMOVED
- **1½** CUPS FROZEN PEAS

1 On wax paper, combine flour, ½ teaspoon salt and pepper. Coat chicken evenly with flour mixture. In large saucepan or Dutch oven, heat oil over medium heat until hot. Add coated chicken; cook, turning, until browned, about 8 to 10 minutes. Remove and set aside.

2 To same saucepan, add remaining ¼ teaspoon salt, garlic, carrots, green onions, potatoes, and rosemary; cook, stirring frequently, until the vegetables begin to brown, about 5 minutes.

3 Add wine; cook 3 minutes. Return chicken to saucepan; add broth. Increase the heat to medium-high; bring to a boil. Reduce heat to low; cover and simmer, turning chicken occasionally until chicken is cooked through and vegetables are tender, about 15 to 20 minutes. Stir in peas; cook, uncovered, until peas are heated through, about 3 minutes.

Calories: 544 · Protein: 41 g
Fat: 12 g/20% calories from fat · Carbohydrate: 56 g
Cholesterol: 94 mg · Sodium: 966 mg

Chicken Thighs with Piquant Sauce

Serves 4

- **3** TABLESPOONS PAPRIKA
- **1½** TEASPOONS DRIED OREGANO
- **¼** TEASPOON PEPPER
- PINCH OF CAYENNE PEPPER
- **8** BONE-IN CHICKEN THIGHS (ABOUT 2½ POUNDS), SKINNED
- **1** TABLESPOON OLIVE OR OTHER VEGETABLE OIL
- **1** MEDIUM ONION, COARSELY CHOPPED
- **2** CLOVES GARLIC, MINCED
- **2** TABLESPOONS ALL-PURPOSE FLOUR
- **½** CUP CHICKEN BROTH, FAT REMOVED
- **¼** CUP RED WINE VINEGAR
- **2** TABLESPOONS TOMATO PASTE
- **½** TEASPOON SUGAR
- **½** TEASPOON SALT

1 In plastic or paper bag, combine paprika, ¾ teaspoon oregano, pepper and cayenne until well mixed. Add chicken; toss to evenly coat.

2 In large skillet, heat oil over medium-high heat until hot. Add chicken; cook, turning occasionally, until chicken begins to darken, about 8 to 10 minutes. Remove chicken and keep warm.

3 To same skillet add onion and garlic; cook, stirring frequently, 1 minute. Add flour; cook, stirring constantly, until flour is incorporated, about 30 seconds. Add remaining ¾ teaspoon oregano, broth, vinegar, tomato paste, sugar and salt until well mixed.

4 Bring to a boil. Return chicken to skillet; bring back to a boil. Cook, turning chicken occasionally, until chicken is cooked through, about 6 minutes. Serve chicken with sauce.

Calories: 306 · Protein: 32 g
Fat: 14 g/43% calories from fat · Carbohydrate: 11 g
Cholesterol: 100 mg · Sodium: 456 mg

Cider-Sautéed Chicken Breasts

Serves 4

- **3** TABLESPOONS ALL-PURPOSE FLOUR
- **½** TEASPOON SALT
- **¼** TEASPOON PEPPER
- **¼** TEASPOON CINNAMON
- **4** SKINLESS, BONELESS CHICKEN BREAST HALVES (ABOUT 1¼ POUNDS)
- **2** TABLESPOONS OLIVE OR OTHER VEGETABLE OIL
- **1** TABLESPOON UNSALTED BUTTER OR MARGARINE
- **¾** TO 1¼ CUPS APPLE CIDER OR JUICE
- **1** SMALL TART UNPEELED GREEN APPLE, CORED AND DICED
- **½** CUP GOLDEN RAISINS
- **2** TABLESPOONS HALF-AND-HALF

1 In plastic or paper bag, combine flour, salt, pepper and cinnamon. Add chicken; toss to evenly coat. Remove chicken and reserve excess seasoned flour mixture.

2 In large skillet, heat oil and butter over medium heat until butter is melted. Add chicken; cook, turning once, until golden, about 8 minutes. Remove chicken and keep warm.

3 To same skillet add reserved seasoned flour; cook, stirring, until light golden, about 2 to 3 minutes. Add ¼ cup cider; cook, stirring, until smooth, about 2 minutes. Add ½ cup cider; check consistency. For thinner sauce add more cider. Increase heat to medium-high. Bring to a boil.

4 Return chicken to skillet; add apple and raisins. Reduce heat to medium-low; cover and simmer until chicken is cooked through, about 5 minutes. Add half-and-half. Serve chicken topped with sauce.

Calories: 429 · Protein: 34 g
Fat: 18 g/39% calories from fat · Carbohydrate: 31 g
Cholesterol: 108 mg · Sodium: 404 mg

Honey-Orange Chicken

Serves 4

2 TABLESPOONS CORNSTARCH
½ TEASPOON SALT
⅛ TEASPOON PEPPER
4 SKINLESS, BONELESS CHICKEN BREAST HALVES (ABOUT 1¼ POUNDS)
2 TABLESPOONS UNSALTED BUTTER OR MARGARINE
½ CUP CHICKEN BROTH, FAT REMOVED
2 TABLESPOONS THAWED FROZEN ORANGE JUICE CONCENTRATE
1 TEASPOON DIJON MUSTARD
½ TEASPOON HONEY

1 In plastic or paper bag, combine cornstarch, salt and pepper. Add chicken; toss to evenly coat. Remove chicken and reserve excess cornstarch mixture.

2 In large skillet, heat 1 tablespoon butter over medium heat until hot. Add chicken; cook on one side until browned, about 5 minutes. Add remaining 1 tablespoon butter; turn chicken and cook until browned, about 5 minutes. Remove chicken and keep warm.

3 In small bowl, combine reserved cornstarch mixture and broth until well mixed. To same skillet add cornstarch-broth mixture, orange juice concentrate, mustard and honey. Bring to a boil, stirring constantly.

4 Return chicken to skillet. Reduce heat to medium-low; cover and simmer until chicken is cooked through, about 5 to 8 minutes. Serve chicken with sauce.

Calories: 272 · Protein: 33 g
Fat: 10 g/37% calories from fat · Carbohydrate: 7 g
Cholesterol: 105 mg · Sodium: 510 mg

Chicken with Garlic-Vinegar Sauce

Serves 4

1 TABLESPOON VEGETABLE OIL
3 TABLESPOONS UNSALTED BUTTER OR MARGARINE
4 LARGE CLOVES GARLIC, UNPEELED
2½ POUNDS CHICKEN PIECES
¼ TEASPOON SALT
½ TEASPOON PEPPER
¼ CUP PLUS 1 TABLESPOON BALSAMIC OR RED WINE VINEGAR
2 MEDIUM TOMATOES, COARSELY CHOPPED
½ CUP CHICKEN BROTH, FAT REMOVED
3 TABLESPOONS CHOPPED PARSLEY

1 In large 12-inch skillet or flameproof casserole, heat oil, 2 tablespoons butter and garlic over medium-high heat until hot. Add chicken; cook, turning once, until browned, about 5 minutes. Season chicken with salt and pepper.

2 To same skillet, add ¼ cup vinegar; bring to a boil. Add tomatoes, broth and 2 tablespoons parsley, stirring to loosen any browned bits. Return mixture to a boil.

3 Reduce heat to low; cover and simmer, turning once, until chicken is cooked through, about 15 minutes. Remove chicken and keep warm.

4 Remove garlic; squeeze from skins and chop. Return to skillet. Add remaining 1 tablespoon vinegar. Increase heat to medium; simmer, stirring constantly, until liquid is reduced by one-third.

5 Add remaining butter to sauce, stirring, until well mixed. Serve chicken topped with sauce.

Calories: 400 · Protein: 42 g
Fat: 23 g/52% calories from fat · Carbohydrate: 5 g
Cholesterol: 150 mg · Sodium: 430 mg

Chicken-Vegetable Stir-Fry

This colorful, tasty stir-fry needs only rice to make it a complete main dish. When brown rice is used, both the taste combination and nutrition are enhanced.

Serves 4

- **3** TABLESPOONS VEGETABLE OIL
- **2** TABLESPOONS SOY SAUCE
- **1** TABLESPOON PLUS 1½ TEASPOONS CORNSTARCH
- **2** SKINLESS, BONELESS CHICKEN BREAST HALVES (ABOUT ¾ POUND), CUT INTO 1-INCH CUBES
- **¾** CUP CHICKEN BROTH, FAT REMOVED
- **½** TEASPOON SUGAR
- **¼** TEASPOON RED PEPPER FLAKES
- **1** LARGE RED PEPPER, CUT INTO 1-INCH SQUARES
- **1** MEDIUM RED ONION, HALVED, CUT INTO ¼-INCH SLICES
- **1** HEAD BROCCOLI (ABOUT 1 POUND), FLORETS REMOVED, STEM CUT INTO ¼-INCH SLICES
- **2** CLOVES GARLIC, MINCED
- **1** CAN (8 OUNCES) SLICED WATER CHESTNUTS, DRAINED
- **¼** CUP WALNUT HALVES OR PIECES

1 In medium bowl, combine 1 tablespoon oil, 1 tablespoon soy sauce and 1 tablespoon cornstarch. Add chicken; toss to evenly coat and let stand.

2 In small bowl, combine broth, sugar, red pepper flakes and remaining 1 tablespoon soy sauce and 1½ teaspoons cornstarch until well mixed.

3 In large skillet or wok, heat 1 tablespoon oil over medium-high heat until hot. Add chicken; cook, stirring constantly, until chicken is opaque but still pink in center. Remove and set aside.

4 To same skillet add remaining 1 tablespoon oil. Add red pepper, onion, broccoli, garlic and water chestnuts; cook, stirring constantly, until onion begins to wilt, about 2 to 3 minutes.

5 Return reserved chicken to skillet; add walnuts and broth-soy mixture. Bring to a boil, stirring constantly, until vegetables are crisp-tender and chicken is cooked through, about 2 to 3 minutes.

PREPARATION TIP

To reduce the amount of sodium in this dish, use "lite" soy sauce or take regular soy sauce and dilute it by one-third with some water or additional chicken broth.

Calories: 295 · Protein: 22 g
Fat: 16 g/48% calories from fat · Carbohydrate: 18 g
Cholesterol: 44 mg · Sodium: 555 mg

Chicken Thighs with Lime and Curry

Serves 4

- **2** TABLESPOONS ALL-PURPOSE FLOUR
- **¼** TEASPOON PEPPER
- **8** BONE-IN CHICKEN THIGHS (ABOUT 2½ POUNDS), SKINNED
- **1** TABLESPOON OLIVE OR OTHER VEGETABLE OIL
- **1** TABLESPOON UNSALTED BUTTER OR MARGARINE
- **1** MEDIUM RED ONION, COARSELY CHOPPED
- **2** CLOVES GARLIC, MINCED
- **½** CUP CHICKEN BROTH, FAT REMOVED
- **1½** TEASPOONS CURRY POWDER
- **3** DROPS HOT PEPPER SAUCE
- **¼** CUP PACKED CILANTRO, CHOPPED
- **¼** CUP LIME JUICE
- **2** TEASPOONS GRATED LIME PEEL
- **⅓** CUP REDUCED-FAT SOUR CREAM

1 In plastic or paper bag, combine flour and pepper until well mixed. Add chicken; toss to evenly coat and reserve excess flour mixture.

2 In large skillet, heat oil and butter over medium-high heat until warm. Add chicken; cook, turning, until golden brown, about 8 to 10 minutes. Remove and keep warm.

3 In same skillet, add onion and garlic; cook, stirring frequently, about 1 minute. Add reserved flour mixture; cook, stirring constantly, until flour is incorporated, about 30 seconds. Add broth, curry powder and hot pepper sauce. Bring to a boil. Reduce heat to low; cover and simmer about 5 minutes.

4 Increase heat to medium-high; bring back to a boil. Add reserved chicken, 2 tablespoons cilantro, lime juice and lime peel; cook until chicken is cooked through, about 5 minutes.

5 Remove from heat; add sour cream until mixed. Serve chicken with sauce and cilantro.

Calories: 345 · Protein: 35 g
Fat: 17 g/45% calories from fat · Carbohydrate: 12 g
Cholesterol: 119 mg · Sodium: 250 mg

Hot and Spicy Chicken with Red Cabbage

Serves 4

- **¼** CUP FINELY CHOPPED PITTED PRUNES
- **2** CLOVES GARLIC, MINCED
- **½** TO 1 TEASPOON RED PEPPER FLAKES
- **2** TABLESPOONS OLIVE OR OTHER VEGETABLE OIL
- **2** SKINLESS, BONELESS CHICKEN BREAST HALVES (ABOUT ¾ POUND), SLICED ACROSS THE GRAIN INTO ½-INCH-WIDE STRIPS
- **8** OUNCES FRESH THIN GREEN BEANS
- **1** TABLESPOON SOY SAUCE
- **1** SMALL HEAD RED CABBAGE, CUT INTO 2-INCH-LONG STRIPS
- **¼** TEASPOON SALT
- **6** GREEN ONIONS, HALVED LENGTHWISE, CUT INTO 2-INCH-LONG PIECES

1 In large shallow dish, combine prunes, garlic, red pepper flakes and 1½ teaspoons oil. Add the chicken and toss to evenly coat. Let stand 30 minutes.

2 In medium saucepan, bring to a boil 3 inches water. Add green beans; cook 1 minute. Rinse under cold water; drain. In medium bowl, combine green beans and soy sauce; set aside.

3 In large skillet or wok, heat 1 tablespoon oil over high heat until hot. Add cabbage and salt; cook, stirring constantly, until cabbage wilts, about 3 minutes. Add green beans with soy sauce and ½ green onions; cook, stirring constantly, about 3 minutes. Transfer to large serving bowl.

4 Reduce heat to medium-high. To same skillet add remaining 1½ teaspoons oil; heat until hot. Add chicken and marinade; cook, stirring constantly, until chicken is no longer pink, about 4 minutes. Return cabbage mixture to skillet; cook until heated through, about 1 minute.

Calories: 243 · Protein: 22 g
Fat: 10 g/36% calories from fat · Carbohydrate: 17 g
Cholesterol: 53 mg · Sodium: 452 mg

Chicken Cutlets with Sour Cream and Jalapeños

Serves 4

- **½** CUP REDUCED-FAT SOUR CREAM
- **½** CUP SHREDDED MONTEREY JACK CHEESE
- **2** TABLESPOONS CHOPPED CILANTRO
- **1** TO 2 JALAPEÑO PEPPERS, SEEDED, IF DESIRED, MINCED
- **4** LARGE SKINLESS, BONELESS CHICKEN BREAST HALVES (ABOUT 1¼ POUNDS), POUNDED ½ INCH THICK
- **¼** TEASPOON SALT
- **¼** TEASPOON PEPPER
- **1** TABLESPOON VEGETABLE OIL
- **1** TABLESPOON UNSALTED BUTTER OR MARGARINE

1 Preheat broiler. Line broiler rack with foil. In small bowl, combine sour cream, cheese, cilantro and jalapeño until well mixed; set aside.

2 Sprinkle both sides of chicken with salt and pepper. In large skillet, heat oil and butter over medium-high heat until butter is melted. Add chicken; cook, turning once, until lightly browned, about 8 to 10 minutes. Transfer chicken to broiler rack.

3 Top each chicken cutlet with a generous spoonful of sour cream mixture. Broil 4 inches from heat source until chicken is cooked through and topping bubbles.

PREPARATION TIP

Serve this tasty cutlet on a hard roll garnished with avocado slices, tomato and lettuce.

Calories: 287 · Protein: 34 g
Fat: 14 g/45% calories from fat · Carbohydrate: 4 g
Cholesterol: 111 mg · Sodium: 288 mg

Chicken Breasts with Apricots and Almonds

Serves 4

- **3** TABLESPOONS ALL-PURPOSE FLOUR
- **2** TEASPOONS CURRY POWDER
- **½** TEASPOON SALT
- **¼** TEASPOON PEPPER
- **4** SKINLESS, BONELESS CHICKEN BREAST HALVES (ABOUT 1¼ POUNDS)
- **1** TABLESPOON OLIVE OR OTHER VEGETABLE OIL
- **1** TABLESPOON BUTTER
- **1** CUP CHICKEN BROTH, FAT REMOVED
- **½** CUP DARK RAISINS
- **2** TABLESPOONS TOMATO PASTE
- **½** TEASPOON SUGAR
- **½** CUP COARSELY CHOPPED DRIED APRICOTS
- **2** GREEN ONIONS, COARSELY CHOPPED
- **½** CUP SLICED ALMONDS, TOASTED

1 In plastic or paper bag, combine flour, 1 teaspoon curry powder, salt and pepper. Add chicken; toss to evenly coat. Remove chicken and reserve 1 tablespoon excess seasoned flour mixture.

2 In large skillet, heat oil and butter over medium-high heat until butter is melted. Add chicken; cook, turning once, until golden, about 8 to 10 minutes. Remove chicken and keep warm.

3 Reduce heat to medium. To same skillet add reserved seasoned flour; cook, stirring, until flour is incorporated, about 30 seconds. Add remaining 1 teaspoon curry powder, broth, raisins, tomato paste and sugar. Increase heat to medium-high. Bring to a boil. Add apricots and reserved chicken.

4 Reduce heat to medium-low; cover and simmer, turning chicken once, until chicken is cooked through, about 5 minutes. Stir in green onions. Serve chicken topped with sauce and toasted almonds.

Calories: 423 · Protein: 38 g
Fat: 17 g/36% calories from fat · Carbohydrate: 29 g
Cholesterol: 97 mg · Sodium: 576 mg

Broiled Garlic-Herb Chicken

Borrowed from the French classic cooking techniques, kneaded butter is used to thicken this sage-flavored sauce.

Serves 4

- **3** TABLESPOONS BUTTER OR MARGARINE, AT ROOM TEMPERATURE
- **3** CLOVES GARLIC, MINCED
- **¼** CUP CHOPPED PARSLEY (OPTIONAL)
- **1½** TEASPOONS DRIED SAGE
- **¼** TEASPOON PEPPER
- **4** BONELESS CHICKEN BREAST HALVES (ABOUT 1¼ POUNDS) WITH SKIN
- **2** TABLESPOONS ALL-PURPOSE FLOUR
- **½** CUP CHICKEN BROTH, FAT REMOVED
- **¼** CUP WATER

1 Preheat broiler. Place chicken on broiler pan; set aside.

2 In small bowl, combine butter, garlic, parsley, if desired, sage and pepper until well mixed. Spread each piece of chicken with ½ teaspoon garlic-sage butter.

3 Broil 4 inches from heat source until golden, about 8 minutes. Turn; spread each piece of chicken with another ½ teaspoon garlic-sage butter. Broil until chicken is cooked through, about 8 to 10 minutes.

4 Meanwhile, with fingers, work flour into remaining garlic-sage butter; set aside.

5 In small skillet or saucepan, combine chicken broth and water over medium-high heat. Bring to a boil. Slowly, bit by bit, add flour-butter mixture into hot broth. Reduce heat to medium-low; simmer 1 minute.

6 Serve sauce over broiled chicken.

PREPARATION TIP

This technique can be used to make other herb sauces. Basically stir or rub together a small amount of butter and flour; then add it slowly to hot broth or pan juices until thickened into a rich smooth sauce.

Calories: 279 · Protein: 28 g
Fat: 16 g/51% calories from fat · Carbohydrate: 4 g
Cholesterol: 101 mg · Sodium: 277 mg

Chicken Breasts with Cilantro Sauce

Serves 4

- **1** TABLESPOON OLIVE OR OTHER VEGETABLE OIL
- **4** SMALL SKINLESS, BONELESS CHICKEN BREAST HALVES (ABOUT 1 POUND)
- **¼** TEASPOON SALT
- **¼** TEASPOON PEPPER
- **1** TEASPOON CORNSTARCH
- **⅓** CUP PLAIN LOW-FAT YOGURT
- **2** TABLESPOONS HALF-AND-HALF
- **¾** CUP CHICKEN BROTH, FAT REMOVED
- **2** TABLESPOONS LEMON JUICE
- **2** CLOVES GARLIC, MINCED
- **2** TABLESPOONS MINCED SHALLOTS
- **1** SMALL TOMATO, SEEDED AND CHOPPED
- **⅓** CUP CHOPPED CILANTRO

1 In large skillet, heat oil over medium-high heat until hot. Add chicken; cook until lightly browned, about 4 minutes. Season chicken with ⅛ teaspoon salt and pepper. Turn; cook until lightly browned, about 4 to 6 minutes. Remove chicken and keep warm.

2 In covered container or jar, combine cornstarch and 1 tablespoon water; shake to mix well. Add yogurt and half-and-half; shake to mix well.

3 To same skillet add broth, lemon juice, garlic and shallots. Reduce heat to low; simmer 30 seconds. Add remaining ⅛ teaspoon salt, tomato and yogurt-cornstarch mixture; cook, stirring constantly, until slightly thickened, about 1 minute. Remove from heat; add cilantro until well mixed. Serve chicken topped with sauce.

Calories: 222 · Protein: 29 g
Fat: 8 g/37% calories from fat · Carbohydrate: 5 g
Cholesterol: 76 mg · Sodium: 369 mg

Pepper-Pecan Chicken

Serves 4

- **2½** POUNDS CHICKEN PIECES
- **½** CUP BUTTERMILK OR PLAIN LOW-FAT YOGURT
- **2** CLOVES GARLIC, PEELED
- **½** CUP PECAN HALVES OR PIECES
- **⅓** CUP UNSEASONED DRIED BREADCRUMBS
- **3** TABLESPOONS COLD UNSALTED BUTTER OR MARGARINE, CUT INTO PIECES
- **½** TEASPOON SALT
- **½** TEASPOON PEPPER
- **2** TABLESPOONS HONEY

1 Preheat oven to 425°. Line broiler pan with foil.

2 In large bowl, combine chicken and buttermilk; toss to evenly coat and set aside.

3 In food processor or blender, process garlic until minced. Add pecans; process until coarsely chopped. Add breadcrumbs, butter, salt and pepper; pulse on and off just until butter is incorporated.

4 Place in shallow bowl or on wax paper. Lightly drain the chicken and add to pecan-breadcrumb mixture and evenly coat.

5 Place skin-side up on prepared pan. Drizzle with honey. Bake 15 minutes.

6 Reduce heat to 375°. Bake until chicken is crisp and cooked through, about 25 minutes.

Calories: 531 · Protein: 45 g
Fat: 29 g/49% calories from fat · Carbohydrate: 22 g
Cholesterol: 152 mg · Sodium: 586 mg

Marinated Garlic-Oregano Chicken

Here the marinade doubles as a flavoring for the chicken and is then thickened to make a flavorful sauce.

Serves 4

- **5** CLOVES GARLIC, MINCED
- **¼** CUP LEMON JUICE
- **1½** TEASPOONS DRIED OREGANO
- **¼** TEASPOON PEPPER
- **4** SKINLESS, BONELESS CHICKEN BREAST HALVES (ABOUT 1¼ POUNDS)
- **¼** CUP CORNSTARCH
- **1** TABLESPOON OLIVE OR OTHER VEGETABLE OIL
- **1** TABLESPOON UNSALTED BUTTER OR MARGARINE
- **1** MEDIUM ONION, CUT INTO THIN WEDGES
- **¾** CUP CHICKEN BROTH, FAT REMOVED
- **½** CUP MINCED GREEN ONION WITH TOPS
- **2½** TEASPOONS GRATED LEMON PEEL
- PINCH OF SUGAR

1 In large shallow baking dish, combine garlic, lemon juice, ¾ teaspoon oregano and pepper. Add chicken; toss to evenly coat. Let stand 10 minutes.

2 On wax paper or shallow dish, place cornstarch. Remove chicken from marinade, reserving remaining marinade. Add chicken to cornstarch; toss to evenly coat and reserve excess cornstarch.

3 In large skillet, heat oil and butter over medium-high heat until butter is melted. Add chicken; cook, turning once, until golden, about 8 to 10 minutes. Remove chicken and keep warm.

4 To same skillet add onion; cook, stirring frequently, until tender, about 2 minutes.

5 In covered container or jar, combine broth and reserved cornstarch; shake to mix well. To same skillet add cornstarch-broth mixture, reserved marinade, remaining ¾ teaspoon oregano, 2 tablespoons green onion, lemon peel and sugar. Bring to a boil.

6 Return chicken to skillet; cook until chicken is cooked through, about 2 to 3 minutes. Serve chicken topped with sauce and sprinkled with remaining green onion.

PREPARATION TIP

When the reserved marinade is added to the skillet, be sure the mixture comes to a full boil.

Calories: 301 · Protein: 35 g
Fat: 11 g/35% calories from fat · Carbohydrate: 13 g
Cholesterol: 97 mg · Sodium: 254 mg

Chicken Thighs Creole

Chicken thighs are one of the least expensive chicken parts. Here they are served in a piquant Louisiana-style tomato sauce.

Serves 4

- **¼** CUP ALL-PURPOSE FLOUR
- **2** TEASPOONS PAPRIKA
- **½** TEASPOON SALT
- **¼** TEASPOON PEPPER
- PINCH OF CAYENNE PEPPER
- **8** CHICKEN THIGHS (ABOUT 2½ POUNDS)
- **2** TABLESPOONS VEGETABLE OIL
- **1** MEDIUM ONION, CHOPPED
- **2** CLOVES GARLIC, MINCED
- **1** MEDIUM GREEN PEPPER, CHOPPED
- **2** RIBS CELERY, CHOPPED
- **½** CUP CHICKEN BROTH, FAT REMOVED
- **1** CUP CANNED CRUSHED TOMATOES
- **1** TEASPOON DRIED THYME

1 In plastic or paper bag, combine flour, paprika, salt, pepper and cayenne pepper. Add chicken thighs; shake to coat chicken well. Remove chicken and reserve the excess flour mixture.

2 In large skillet, heat 1 tablespoon oil over medium-high heat until hot. Add chicken thighs; cook, turning occasionally, until light golden, about 8 minutes. Remove and keep warm.

3 To same skillet add onion, garlic, green pepper and celery; cook, stirring, 1 minute. Add 1 tablespoon reserved flour mixture; cook, stirring, until flour is incorporated, about 30 seconds.

4 Add chicken broth, tomatoes and thyme. Increase heat to medium-high; bring to a boil. Add reserved chicken thighs; bring back to a boil. Reduce heat to medium-low; cover and simmer until chicken thighs are cooked through, about 15 minutes.

PREPARATION TIP

To round out the meal, serve the chicken creole over rice cooked in chicken broth and tossed with toasted almonds.

Calories: 854 · Protein: 48 g
Fat: 49 g/51% calories from fat · Carbohydrate: 55 g
Cholesterol: 189 mg · Sodium: 936 mg

Quick Curry-Roasted Chicken

Serves 4

- **1** WHOLE CHICKEN (2½ POUNDS)
- **¾** TEASPOON CURRY POWDER
- **½** TEASPOON SALT
- **1** TABLESPOON OLIVE OR OTHER VEGETABLE OIL
- **¼** TEASPOON PEPPER

1 Preheat oven to 425°. Line baking pan with foil.

2 With poultry shears, cut along either side of backbone and remove. With chicken halves breast-side up, flatten with heel of hand. Cut off wing tips.

3 In small bowl, combine curry powder and salt. Rub chicken, inside and out, with 1½ teaspoons oil. Add remaining 1½ teaspoons oil to curry mixture to make paste. Rub paste on both sides of chicken. Sprinkle with pepper.

4 Place chicken skin-side up in prepared pan. Bake until chicken is cooked through, about 45 to 55 minutes. To serve, let stand 5 minutes then cut in quarters.

PREPARATION TIP

Other spices or herbs can be used in place of curry powder—cinnamon, oregano, basil, cumin—using the same method.

Calories: 407 · Protein: 57 g
Fat: 18 g/42% calories from fat · Carbohydrate: 0 g
Cholesterol: 177 mg · Sodium: 437 mg

Lemon-Stuffed Roasted Chicken

Serves 4

- **4** TABLESPOONS UNSALTED BUTTER OR MARGARINE, MELTED
- **4** GREEN ONIONS, COARSELY CHOPPED
- **3** CLOVES GARLIC, MINCED
- **3** TEASPOONS DRIED BASIL
- **½** TEASPOON PEPPER
- **1** WHOLE CHICKEN (3 POUNDS)
- **½** TEASPOON SALT
- **3** LEMONS, 2 PIERCED SEVERAL TIMES WITH A FORK AND HALVED, 1 THINLY SLICED

1 Preheat oven to 425°.

2 In small bowl, combine the butter, green onions, garlic, 2 teaspoons basil and ¼ teaspoon pepper.

3 Place chicken on rack in roasting pan.

4 Sprinkle chicken cavity with remaining 1 teaspoon basil, remaining ¼ teaspoon pepper and salt; then stuff the lemon halves into the chicken cavity.

5 Place lemon slices over chicken; spoon some butter mixture over lemon and chicken. Bake 15 minutes.

6 Reduce heat to 350°; bake until juices run clear, about 45 minutes, basting every 15 minutes with remaining butter mixture.

7 To serve, let stand 5 minutes; carve and serve with pan juices.

Calories: 433 · Protein: 49 g
Fat: 24 g/51 calories from fat · Carbohydrate: 2 g
Cholesterol: 183 mg · Sodium: 510 mg

Barbecued Chicken with Tropical Fruit Salsa

Unlike the salsa made of a tomato and onion base, this salsa is made with the fruit of the pineapple and mango.

Serves 4

- **1** CAN (20 OUNCES) CRUSHED PINEAPPLE IN PINEAPPLE JUICE
- **1** MANGO, DICED
- **¼** CUP CHOPPED FRESH CILANTRO OR PARSLEY
- **¼** CUP CHOPPED MANGO CHUTNEY
- **2** TABLESPOONS FRESH LEMON JUICE
- **½** TEASPOON SALT
- **¼** CUP KETCHUP
- **2** TEASPOONS OLIVE OR OTHER VEGETABLE OIL
- **½** TEASPOON DRIED OREGANO
- **¼** TEASPOON ALLSPICE
- **⅛** TEASPOON GROUND CLOVES
- **⅛** TEASPOON CAYENNE PEPPER
- **4** SKINLESS, BONELESS CHICKEN BREAST HALVES (ABOUT 1¼ POUNDS)

1 Drain pineapple, reserving ¼ cup juice. In large bowl, combine crushed pineapple, mango, cilantro, chutney, lemon juice and ¼ teaspoon salt.

2 In small bowl, combine reserved pineapple juice, remaining salt, ketchup, oil, oregano, allspice, cloves and cayenne. Stir 1 tablespoon spiced ketchup into pineapple-mango mixture. Cover and refrigerate until serving time.

3 In sturdy plastic bag or shallow bowl, place remaining spiced ketchup. Add chicken; cover or seal tightly and refrigerate 30 minutes or up to 2 hours.

4 Prepare broiler or grill according to manufacturer's directions. Broil or grill chicken 4 inches from heat source until lightly browned, about 4 minutes. Turn; broil or grill until chicken is thoroughly cooked, about 4 to 6 minutes.

5 Slice chicken into thin strips and serve topped with tropical fruit salsa.

PREPARATION TIP

Be careful when grilling or broiling the chicken, the sugar in the pineapple juice and ketchup burn quickly if the flame flares up.

Calories: 341 · Protein: 34 g
Fat: 7 g/19% calories from fat · Carbohydrate: 35 g
Cholesterol: 89 mg · Sodium: 357 mg

Crispy Oven-Fried Chicken

Serves 4

- **2** CLOVES GARLIC, PEELED
- **4** SLICES WHITE BREAD, TORN INTO PIECES
- **¼** CUP GRATED PARMESAN CHEESE (ABOUT 1 OUNCE)
- **1** TEASPOON DRIED CRUMBLED SAGE OR THYME
- **½** TEASPOON SALT
- **¼** TEASPOON PEPPER
- **2** TABLESPOONS BUTTER OR MARGARINE, CUT INTO SMALL PIECES
- **¼** CUP MILK
- **2½** POUNDS CHICKEN PIECES

1 Preheat oven to 375°. Line baking pan with foil.

2 To make breading, in food processor or blender, process garlic until finely chopped. Add bread, Parmesan, sage, salt and pepper; process, pulsing machine on and off, until bread is finely crumbed. Add butter; process until butter is completely incorporated. Transfer to plastic or paper bag.

3 Place milk in shallow bowl. To coat, dip chicken pieces in milk, a few at a time, then in bag; shake to coat chicken well.

4 Place the coated chicken on prepared pan. Bake until coating is crisp and juices run clear when chicken is pierced with a fork, about 45 to 55 minutes.

PREPARATION TIP

The breading can be made ahead and stored in the refrigerator until ready to use. As long as you're making it, double or triple the recipe to have on hand.

Calories: 449 · Protein: 39 g
Fat: 26 g/52% calories from fat · Carbohydrate: 14 g
Cholesterol: 132 mg · Sodium: 657 mg

Roasted Chicken Oriental-Style

Serves 4

- **3** TABLESPOONS SOY SAUCE
- **3** TABLESPOONS KETCHUP
- **1** TABLESPOON LIGHT BROWN SUGAR
- **1½** TEASPOONS ORIENTAL SESAME OIL
- **2** CLOVES GARLIC, MINCED
- **2½** POUNDS CHICKEN PIECES

1 Preheat oven to 375°. Line baking pan with foil. In small bowl, combine soy sauce, ketchup, brown sugar, sesame oil and garlic until well mixed.

2 Place chicken pieces skin-side up in baking pan. Add soy sauce mixture; toss to evenly coat and let stand 10 minutes.

3 Bake until chicken is cooked through, about 35 to 40 minutes, basting occasionally with pan juices.

Calories: 365 · Protein: 50 g
Fat: 14 g/36% calories from fat · Carbohydrate: 6 g
Cholesterol: 152 mg · Sodium: 922 mg

Stovetop Barbecued Burgers

Serves 4

- **1** POUND GROUND CHICKEN
- **2** TEASPOONS OLIVE OR OTHER VEGETABLE OIL
- **2** CLOVES GARLIC, MINCED
- **1** MEDIUM ONION, CHOPPED
- **1** CUP CRUSHED TOMATOES
- **¼** CUP KETCHUP
- **2** TABLESPOONS THAWED FROZEN ORANGE JUICE CONCENTRATE
- **1** TABLESPOON CHILI POWDER
- **¼** TEASPOON PEPPER

1 Form ground chicken into 4 even patties, about 3½ inches in diameter. In large skillet, heat oil over medium-high heat until hot. Add burgers; cook until browned, about 5 minutes. Turn; cook until browned, about 4 minutes. Remove and keep warm.

2 To same skillet add garlic and onion; cook, stirring, until onion is tender, about 5 minutes. Add tomatoes, ketchup, orange juice concentrate, chili powder and pepper. Bring to a boil. Cook 1 minute.

3 Return burgers to skillet; cook until heated through, about 1 to 2 minutes. Serve burgers topped with sauce.

PREPARATION TIP
If preferred, the burgers can be broiled or grilled and the sauce made separately, as directed, in the skillet. Add cooked burgers to skillet to coat with barbecue sauce.

Calories: 252 · Protein: 21 g
Fat: 13 g/47% calories from fat · Carbohydrate: 11 g
Cholesterol: 107 mg · Sodium: 74 mg

Herbed Chicken Breasts with Lentils

Serves 4

- **½** TEASPOON DRIED THYME
- **½** TEASPOON DRIED ROSEMARY
- **¼** TEASPOON SALT
- **4** SMALL SKINLESS, BONELESS CHICKEN BREAST HALVES (ABOUT 1 POUND)
- **1** CUP RED LENTILS
- **1** CUP CHICKEN BROTH, FAT REMOVED
- **3** CLOVES GARLIC, MINCED
- **¼** TEASPOON GROUND ALLSPICE
- **¼** TEASPOON GROUND CINNAMON
- **¼** TEASPOON GROUND GINGER
- **2** GREEN ONIONS, FINELY CHOPPED

1 Preheat broiler or grill according to manufacturer's directions. In small bowl, combine thyme, rosemary and salt. Rub herb mixture over chicken and let stand.

2 In large saucepan, combine lentils, broth, garlic, allspice, cinnamon and ginger over medium-high heat. Bring to a boil. Reduce heat to low; cover and simmer until lentils are crunchy, about 5 minutes. Add green onions.

3 Broil or grill chicken 4 inches from heat source, turning once, until chicken is cooked through, about 8 to 10 minutes. Serve chicken on bed of lentils.

PREPARATION TIP
Regular lentils may be substituted, but increase cooking time by about 25 to 40 minutes or until lentils are tender.

Calories: 324 · Protein: 41 g
Fat: 4 g/13% calories from fat · Carbohydrate: 28 g
Cholesterol: 71 mg · Sodium: 665 mg

Chicken Quesadillas

Serves 4

- **2** SKINLESS, BONELESS CHICKEN BREAST HALVES (ABOUT ¾ POUND)
- **3** TABLESPOONS LIME JUICE
- **8** MEDIUM (8-INCH) FLOUR TORTILLAS
- **¾** CUP SHREDDED MONTEREY JACK CHEESE (3 OUNCES)
- **½** CUP CHOPPED FRESH CILANTRO (OPTIONAL)
- **4** GREEN ONIONS, THINLY SLICED
- **½** CUP MILD OR MEDIUM-HOT PREPARED SALSA

1 In small bowl, combine chicken and lime juice; toss to evenly coat.

2 Preheat broiler or grill according to manufacturer's directions.

3 Broil or grill the chicken until it is slightly browned, about 4 minutes. Turn; broil or grill until chicken is cooked through, about 4 to 6 minutes. Remove; when slightly cool, cut into thin slices.

4 Fold four 24-inch lengths heavy-duty foil in half to form 12-inch by 18-inch rectangle. Spray with nonstick cooking spray.

5 Place 1 tortilla in center of each. Place ¼ each chicken, cheese, cilantro, if desired, green onions and salsa. Top with remaining tortillas. Tightly seal packets.

6 Broil or grill the chicken 4 inches from heat source, turning once, until piping hot, about 5 minutes.

7 Carefully open the packets, cut each into quarters.

Calories: 416 · Protein: 30 g
Fat: 14 g/31% calories from fat · Carbohydrate: 43 g
Cholesterol: 73 mg · Sodium: 542 mg

Tomato-Tarragon Braised Chicken

Serves 4

- **3** TABLESPOONS ALL-PURPOSE FLOUR
- **½** TEASPOON PEPPER
- **4** BONE-IN CHICKEN BREAST HALVES (ABOUT 2½ POUNDS)
- **1** TABLESPOON OLIVE OR OTHER VEGETABLE OIL
- **8** MEDIUM SHALLOTS, PEELED
- **2** CLOVES GARLIC, MINCED
- **1** CUP CRUSHED TOMATOES
- **½** CUP CHICKEN BROTH, FAT REMOVED
- **3** TABLESPOONS MINCED FRESH OR 1 TEASPOON DRIED TARRAGON
- **1** TEASPOON LIGHT BROWN SUGAR

1 In plastic of paper bag, combine flour and pepper until well mixed. Add chicken; toss to evenly coat. Remove chicken and reserve excess seasoned flour.

2 In large skillet, heat oil over medium-high heat until hot. Add chicken, skin-side down; cook until golden, about 6 minutes. Turn; cook 3 minutes. Remove and keep warm.

3 To same skillet add reserved seasoned flour; stir until flour is no longer visible. Add shallots, garlic, tomatoes, broth, tarragon and brown sugar. Bring to a boil.

4 Return chicken to skillet. Reduce heat to low; cover and simmer, turning occasionally, until chicken is cooked through, about 15 to 20 minutes.

Calories: 223 · Protein: 28 g
Fat: 7 g/31% calories from fat · Carbohydrate: 9 g
Cholesterol: 71 mg · Sodium: 168 mg

Chicken with Chili Corn Sauce

Just a touch of sour cream nicely cools the slightly spicy corn sauce for these chili-rubbed chicken breasts.

Serves 4

- **2** TEASPOONS MEDIUM-HOT CHILI POWDER
- **½** TEASPOON SALT
- **¼** TEASPOON SUGAR
- **4** SKINLESS, BONELESS CHICKEN BREAST HALVES (ABOUT 1¼ POUNDS)
- **¾** CUP REDUCED-SODIUM CHICKEN BROTH, FAT REMOVED
- **1** RED PEPPER, DICED
- **1** GREEN PEPPER, DICED
- **¾** CUP FROZEN WHOLE-KERNEL CORN
- **2** TABLESPOONS FINELY CHOPPED GREEN ONIONS
- **2** TABLESPOONS LIME JUICE
- **2** TABLESPOONS LIGHT SOUR CREAM

1 Preheat broiler or grill according to manufacturer's directions. In small bowl, combine ½ teaspoon chili powder, ¼ teaspoon salt and sugar. Rub on chicken and let stand.

2 In large nonstick skillet, combine remaining 1½ teaspoons chili powder and ¼ teaspoon salt, broth, peppers, corn, green onions and lime juice over medium-high heat. Bring to a boil. Reduce heat to low; simmer, until sauce is slightly thickened, about 7 minutes.

3 Meanwhile, broil or grill chicken 4 inches from heat source until chicken is browned, about 4 minutes. Turn; broil or grill until chicken is cooked through, about 4 to 6 minutes.

4 Add sour cream to corn mixture until well mixed. Serve chicken topped with corn mixture.

PREPARATION TIP

For easier last-minute preparation, make the corn sauce ahead without the sour cream. At serving time gently reheat; then when off the heat, stir in sour cream to prevent curdling.

Calories: 187 · Protein: 29 g
Fat: 3 g/14% calories from fat · Carbohydrate: 11 g
Cholesterol: 68 mg · Sodium: 482 mg

Brunswick Stew

Serves 4

- **1** TABLESPOON PEANUT OR OTHER VEGETABLE OIL
- **1½** POUNDS CHICKEN PIECES
- **1** POUND SMOKED HAM HOCKS
- **½** CAN (16 OUNCES) NO-SALT-ADDED TOMATOES
- **2** MEDIUM PLUM TOMATOES, CHOPPED
- **1** LARGE ALL-PURPOSE POTATO, CUT INTO 1-INCH CUBES
- **1** MEDIUM ONION, CUT INTO WEDGES
- **4** CUPS SHREDDED CABBAGE (ABOUT ¼ MEDIUM HEAD)
- **½** PACKAGE (10 OUNCES) FROZEN LIMA BEANS
- **¾** CUP FROZEN OR DRAINED CANNED WHOLE-KERNEL CORN
- **1** MEDIUM GREEN PEPPER, CUT INTO 1-INCH PIECES

1 In large saucepan or Dutch oven, heat oil over medium-high heat until warm. Add chicken; cook, turning, until golden brown, about 10 minutes.

2 Add ham hock, tomatoes and enough water to cover ingredients. Bring to a boil. Reduce heat to low; cover and simmer until chicken is tender, about 20 to 25 minutes. Remove chicken; when cool enough to handle skin, bone and cut into bite-size pieces.

3 Cover and continue to simmer 1 hour. Add potato, onion and cabbage. Increase heat to medium-low; cover and simmer until potato is almost tender, about 15 minutes. Add lima beans, corn and green pepper; cover and simmer 10 minutes.

4 Remove ham hock; when cool enough to handle, cut meat into bite-size pieces. Return cut-up chicken and ham to saucepan. Cook, uncovered, until heated through, about 5 minutes.

Calories: 453 · Protein: 41 g
Fat: 18 g/35% calories from fat · Carbohydrate: 32 g
Cholesterol: 115 mg · Sodium: 488 mg

Chicken Jambalaya

Serves 4

- **1** TABLESPOON OLIVE OR OTHER VEGETABLE OIL
- **2** CLOVES GARLIC, MINCED
- **1** LARGE ONION, FINELY CHOPPED
- **1** GREEN PEPPER, DICED
- **2** OUNCES CANADIAN BACON, COARSELY CHOPPED
- **1** CUP CHICKEN BROTH, FAT REMOVED
- **1¼** CUPS LONG-GRAIN RICE
- **1** CUP DRY WHITE WINE
- **1½** CUPS WATER
- **1** TEASPOON DRIED ROSEMARY
- **½** TEASPOON SALT
- **¼** TEASPOON ALLSPICE
- **1** POUND SKINLESS, BONELESS CHICKEN THIGHS, CUT INTO 1½-INCH PIECES
- **1** POUND PLUM TOMATOES, COARSELY CHOPPED
- **1** PACKAGE (10 OUNCES) FROZEN WHOLE OKRA, THAWED

1 In large saucepan or Dutch oven, heat oil over medium heat until warm. Add garlic and onion; cook, stirring occasionally, until onion is tender, about 5 minutes. Add green pepper, bacon and ¼ cup broth; cook, stirring occasionally, until pepper is tender, about 5 minutes.

2 Add rice, stirring to coat. Add wine; cook until wine has evaporated, about 5 minutes. Add remaining ¾ cup broth, water, rosemary, salt and allspice. Increase heat to medium-high. Bring to a boil. Reduce heat to low; cover and simmer 10 minutes.

3 Stir in chicken, tomatoes and okra. Increase heat to medium-high. Bring to a boil. Reduce heat to low; cover and simmer until chicken is cooked through and rice is tender, about 10 minutes.

Calories: 526 · Protein: 37 g
Fat: 9 g/16% calories from fat · Carbohydrate: 62 g
Cholesterol: 78 mg · Sodium: 743 mg

Salsa-Marinated Chicken

Serves 6

1½ CUPS PREPARED SALSA
2 TABLESPOONS NO-SALT-ADDED TOMATO PASTE
4 SKINLESS, BONELESS CHICKEN BREAST HALVES (ABOUT 1¼ POUNDS)
1 GREEN PEPPER, CUT INTO THIN STRIPS
⅔ CUP FROZEN WHOLE-KERNEL CORN, THAWED
3 TABLESPOONS FINELY CHOPPED GREEN ONION
2 TABLESPOONS LIME JUICE
2 TABLESPOONS CHOPPED FRESH CILANTRO OR PARSLEY

1 Preheat broiler or grill according to manufacturer's directions. In shallow bowl, combine ½ cup salsa and tomato paste until well mixed. Add chicken; toss to evenly coat and set aside.

2 In medium bowl, combine remaining 1 cup salsa, green pepper, corn, green onion, lime juice and cilantro.

3 Broil or grill chicken 4 inches from heat source until chicken is browned, about 4 minutes. Turn; broil or grill until chicken is cooked through, about 4 to 6 minutes. Serve chicken with vegetable mixture.

PREPARATION TIP
For economy, use less expensive chicken parts, such as chicken legs, just the thighs or wings.

Calories: 182 · Protein: 27 g
Fat: 2 g/10% calories from fat · Carbohydrate: 14 g
Cholesterol: 66 mg · Sodium: 530 mg

Onion-Smothered Chicken

Serves 4

6 TABLESPOONS RED WINE VINEGAR
4 TEASPOONS SUGAR
½ TEASPOON SAGE
½ TEASPOON SALT
4 SKINLESS, BONELESS CHICKEN BREAST HALVES (ABOUT 1¼ POUNDS)
2 TEASPOONS OLIVE OR OTHER VEGETABLE OIL
2 LARGE ONIONS, HALVED AND THINLY SLICED
1 CUP CHICKEN BROTH, FAT REMOVED
1 TABLESPOON ALL-PURPOSE FLOUR
1 MEDIUM CARROT, CUT INTO THIN STRIPS
1 RED PEPPER, CUT INTO THIN STRIPS
¼ TEASPOON PEPPER

1 In shallow bowl, combine 3 tablespoons vinegar, 2 teaspoons sugar, ¼ teaspoon sage and ¼ teaspoon salt until well mixed. Add chicken; toss to evenly coat. Cover and refrigerate.

2 In large skillet, heat oil over medium heat until warm. Add onions and remaining 2 teaspoons sugar; cook, stirring occasionally, until onions begin to brown, about 5 minutes. Add broth; cook until most of liquid has evaporated, about 5 minutes. Add remaining 3 tablespoons vinegar, ¼ teaspoon salt and ¼ teaspoon sage, flour, carrot, red pepper and pepper; cook until onions are tender and caramelized, about 10 minutes.

3 Prepare broiler or grill according to manufacturer's directions. Broil or grill chicken 4 inches from heat source until lightly browned, about 4 minutes. Turn; broil or grill until chicken is thoroughly cooked, about 4 to 6 minutes.

4 Serve chicken surrounded by onion mixture.

Calories: 298 · Protein: 35 g
Fat: 10 g/30% calories from fat · Carbohydrate: 15 g
Cholesterol: 90 mg · Sodium: 551 mg

Sweet-and-Sour Baked Chicken

Fresh apples and plums provide a part of the sweetness in this chicken dish that contrasts tart cider vinegar with brown sugar.

Serves 4

2½ POUNDS CHICKEN PIECES
1 TABLESPOON OLIVE OR OTHER VEGETABLE OIL
2 TEASPOONS DRIED TARRAGON
½ TEASPOON SALT
½ TEASPOON PEPPER
2 TABLESPOONS BUTTER OR MARGARINE
1 SMALL ONION, COARSELY CHOPPED
2 TABLESPOONS ALL-PURPOSE FLOUR
1⅓ CUPS CHICKEN BROTH
2 TABLESPOONS CIDER VINEGAR
2 TEASPOONS BROWN SUGAR
1 LARGE APPLE, CORED, CUT INTO ¼-INCH WEDGES
2 PLUMS, PITTED, CUT INTO ¼-INCH WEDGES

1 Preheat oven to 425°. Place chicken in roasting pan large enough to hold in single layer; set aside.

2 In small bowl, combine oil, 1 teaspoon tarragon, salt and pepper. Brush over chicken. Bake 15 minutes. Reduce heat to 375°; bake until chicken is cooked through, about 25 minutes.

3 In medium skillet, heat butter over medium heat until melted. Add onion; cook until tender, about 4 minutes. Add flour; cook, stirring, until flour is incorporated, about 30 seconds. Add remaining 1 teaspoon tarragon, chicken broth, vinegar and brown sugar. Bring to a boil. Reduce heat to low; cover and simmer while chicken cooks.

4 About 10 minutes before chicken is done, increase heat to medium. Add apple and plums; cook until fruit is just tender, about 7 to 9 minutes. Pour over chicken; toss gently to evenly coat.

PREPARATION TIP

Depending on the visual appearance desired, any variety of plums can be used—blue-black Friars, ruby-skinned Larodas, jade-green Kelseys or frosty-purple Italian prune plums.

Calories: 577 · Protein: 38 g
Fat: 39 g/60% calories from fat · Carbohydrate: 18 g
Cholesterol: 160 mg · Sodium: 795 mg

Broiled Chicken with Tomato Butter

Here the intense tomato flavor of sun-dried tomatoes is combined with the richness of butter for an easy, delicious dish.

Serves 4

- **¼** CUP LEMON JUICE
- **4** SKINLESS, BONELESS CHICKEN BREAST HALVES (ABOUT 1¼ POUNDS)
- **3** SUN-DRIED TOMATO HALVES
- **½** CUP BOILING WATER
- **2** GREEN ONIONS, CUT INTO 1-INCH PIECES
- **2** TABLESPOONS UNSALTED BUTTER OR MARGARINE, AT ROOM TEMPERATURE
- **2** TEASPOONS GRATED LEMON PEEL
- PINCH OF DRY MUSTARD
- PINCH OF WHITE PEPPER
- PINCH OF RED PEPPER FLAKES

1 In medium bowl, combine lemon juice and chicken; toss to evenly coat. In small bowl, combine sun-dried tomatoes and water. Let stand until tomatoes are softened, about 5 minutes. Drain.

2 Preheat broiler. Line broiler pan with foil.

3 In food processor or blender, process softened sun-dried tomatoes and green onions. Add butter, lemon peel, mustard, pepper and red pepper flakes; process until well mixed. In small skillet, place ½ tomato butter over low heat until melted.

4 Meanwhile, on wax paper or plastic wrap, shape remaining tomato butter into a log; refrigerate until serving time.

5 Arrange chicken on prepared pan; brush with melted tomato butter. Broil 4 inches from heat source until chicken is browned, about 4 minutes. Turn; brush with melted tomato butter. Broil until chicken is browned and cooked through, about 4 to 6 minutes.

6 Cut cold tomato butter into 8 slices; serve each chicken breast half topped with 2 slices.

PREPARATION TIP

For longer storage, place the tomato butter log in the freezer for up to 1 month. Slice and use as needed to top vegetables and meats.

Calories: 253 · Protein: 33 g
Fat: 10 g/39% calories from fat · Carbohydrate: 4 g
Cholesterol: 105 mg · Sodium: 136 mg

Marinated Chicken Legs

Serves 4

- **¾** CUP MALT VINEGAR
- **½** CUP DRY WHITE WINE
- **2** LARGE SHALLOTS, THINLY SLICED
- **2** TEASPOONS GROUND MACE
- **⅛** TEASPOON PEPPER
- **2** TABLESPOONS CHOPPED FRESH OR 2 TEASPOONS DRIED BASIL
- **4** WHOLE CHICKEN LEGS, SKINNED (ABOUT 1¼ POUNDS)
- **¼** TEASPOON SALT

1 In small saucepan, combine vinegar, wine, shallots, mace, pepper and basil over medium heat. Bring to a simmer; cook 2 minutes. Sprinkle chicken with salt; place in sturdy plastic bag or shallow bowl. Add vinegar mixture; cover or seal tightly and refrigerate 8 hours or overnight.

2 Prepare broiler or grill according to manufacturer's directions. Broil or grill chicken until browned, about 10 minutes. Turn; broil or grill until chicken is cooked through, about 10 to 12 minutes.

PREPARATION TIP
Mace comes from the same plant as nutmeg. It is the delicate lacy fiber that coats the nutmeg kernel. If you don't have mace, nutmeg or allspice can be substituted.

Calories: 177 · Protein: 19 g
Fat: 7 g/35% calories from fat · Carbohydrate: 4 g
Cholesterol: 65 mg · Sodium: 201 mg

Chicken Zucchini Stew

Serves 4

- **1** CAN (28 OUNCES) NO-SALT-ADDED WHOLE TOMATOES, COARSELY CHOPPED
- **1½** CUPS CHICKEN BROTH, FAT REMOVED
- **2** CLOVES GARLIC, MINCED
- **1** TEASPOON DRIED BASIL
- **1** TEASPOON SUGAR
- **½** TO ¾ TEASPOON CHILI POWDER
- **½** TEASPOON SALT
- **¼** TEASPOON PEPPER
- **2** SKINLESS, BONELESS CHICKEN BREAST HALVES (ABOUT ¾ POUND), CUT INTO BITE-SIZE PIECES
- **8** OUNCES WIDE EGG NOODLES, SLIGHTLY UNDERCOOKED
- **2** MEDIUM ZUCCHINI, CUT INTO THIN COINS

1 In large saucepan or Dutch oven, combine tomatoes, broth, garlic, basil, sugar, chili powder, salt and pepper over medium heat. Bring to a simmer; cook, stirring occasionally, about 10 minutes.

2 Add chicken. Reduce heat to low; cover and simmer until chicken is cooked, about 8 to 10 minutes. Add noodles and zucchini. Cook until noodles and zucchini are tender, about 5 minutes.

PREPARATION TIP
Divide into individual serving dishes and freeze. Thaw, then reheat in microwave, or covered in the oven or on top of the stove.

Calories: 379 · Protein: 30 g
Fat: 6 g/14% calories from fat · Carbohydrate: 49 g
Cholesterol: 104 mg · Sodium: 629 mg

Szechwan Chicken Wings

Great do-ahead picnic finger food or easy summer dinner, these marinated chicken wings are tart, hot and golden brown.

Serves 4

- **2** TANGERINES OR 1 ORANGE
- **3** SLICES ¼-INCH-THICK FRESH GINGER
- **3** CLOVES GARLIC, MINCED
- **2** GREEN ONIONS, FINELY CHOPPED
- **⅓** CUP REDUCED-SODIUM SOY SAUCE
- **2** TABLESPOONS ORIENTAL SESAME OIL
- **1** TABLESPOON HONEY
- **¾** TEASPOON RED PEPPER FLAKES
- **12** CHICKEN WINGS
- **2** TEASPOONS CORNSTARCH

1 Grate peel from tangerines and measure out 1½ teaspoons; juice tangerines and measure out ⅓ cup.

2 In large shallow dish or casserole, combine tangerine peel and juice, ginger, garlic, green onions, soy sauce, oil, honey and red pepper flakes until well mixed. Add chicken wings; toss to evenly coat. Cover and let stand 30 minutes or refrigerate overnight.

3 Preheat broiler. Line broiler pan with foil. Place wings on prepared pan, reserving marinade. Broil 4 inches from heat source until browned, about 7 to 10 minutes. Turn; broil until crisp and well browned, about 7 to 10 minutes.

4 Meanwhile, pour reserved marinade into saucepan over medium heat. Stir in cornstarch until well mixed. Bring to a boil, stirring constantly. Reduce heat to low; simmer, stirring occasionally, until thickened. Serve sauce with chicken wings.

PREPARATION TIP

Marinate the chicken wings the day before and these spicy wings will be ready to go on the table in 20 minutes; or make the entire recipe in advance and serve cold with deli potato salad.

Calories: 438 · Protein: 32 g
Fat: 29 g/59% calories from fat · Carbohydrate: 11 g
Cholesterol: 95 mg · Sodium: 886 mg

Make-Ahead Chicken Newburg

Serves 6

- **1** CUP CHICKEN BROTH, FAT REMOVED
- **½** CUP DRY SHERRY
- **3** TABLESPOONS ALL-PURPOSE FLOUR
- **1** TEASPOON BROWN SUGAR
- **4** LARGE SKINLESS, BONELESS CHICKEN BREAST HALVES (ABOUT 1½ POUNDS), CUT INTO 1-INCH CHUNKS
- **8** OUNCES BOILED HAM, CUT INTO THICK MATCHSTICK PIECES
- **2** TABLESPOONS OLIVE OR OTHER VEGETABLE OIL
- **1½** TEASPOONS DRIED ROSEMARY, CRUMBLED
- **¼** TEASPOON PEPPER
- **1** TABLESPOON UNSALTED BUTTER OR MARGARINE
- **1** POUND SMALL MUSHROOMS

1 In small covered container or jar, combine broth, 6 tablespoons sherry, flour and ½ teaspoon brown sugar. Shake until well mixed; refrigerate until ready to use.

2 In medium bowl, combine chicken, ham, remaining 2 tablespoons sherry, remaining ½ teaspoon sugar, 1 tablespoon oil, rosemary and pepper; toss gently to evenly coat. Cover and refrigerate 30 minutes or up to 24 hours.

3 In large skillet, heat remaining 1 tablespoon oil and butter over medium-high heat until butter is melted. Add mushrooms; cook, stirring frequently, until wilted, about 5 minutes. Add chicken and marinade; cook, stirring frequently, until chicken is almost cooked, about 8 to 10 minutes.

4 Shake broth-sherry mixture; add to chicken-mushroom mixture. Bring to a boil; cook, stirring constantly, until sauce has thickened and chicken is cooked through, about 2 to 3 minutes.

Calories: 283 · Protein: 28 g
Fat: 11 g/37% calories from fat · Carbohydrate: 9 g
Cholesterol: 72 mg · Sodium: 767 mg

Lime-Grilled Chicken Sandwiches

Serves 4

- **¼** CUP LIME JUICE
- **1** TABLESPOON OLIVE OR OTHER VEGETABLE OIL
- **½** TEASPOON SALT
- **¼** TEASPOON PEPPER
- **4** CHICKEN CUTLETS (ABOUT 1 POUND), POUNDED ¼ INCH THICK
- **⅓** CUP MAYONNAISE
- **2** TABLESPOONS CHOPPED CILANTRO (OPTIONAL)
- **1** TEASPOON GRATED LIME PEEL (OPTIONAL)
- **1** SMALL AVOCADO, PEELED AND SLICED
- **4** CLUB OR OTHER HARD ROLLS, CUT IN HALF LENGTHWISE
- **4** LETTUCE LEAVES
- **¼** CUP CRANBERRY SAUCE

1 Prepare broiler or grill according to manufacturer's directions. In shallow bowl, combine 2 tablespoons lime juice, oil, salt and pepper until well mixed. Add cutlets; toss to evenly coat.

2 Broil or grill 4 inches from heat source, turning once, until cooked through, about 6 minutes. Meanwhile, in small bowl, combine 1 tablespoon lime juice, mayonnaise, cilantro and lime peel, if desired; set aside.

3 Toss avocado with remaining lime juice. Broil or grill rolls until lightly toasted, about 30 seconds.

4 To serve, spread both sides of rolls with lime mayonnaise; layer ¼ each lettuce, chicken cutlet, avocado slices and 1 tablespoon cranberry sauce.

Calories: 613 · Protein: 30 g
Fat: 39 g/58% calories from fat · Carbohydrate: 33 g
Cholesterol: 87 mg · Sodium: 731 mg

Chicken with Red Chili Sauce

A wonderful example of the combining of a marinade of soy sauce and ginger with a hot sauce of red pepper flakes.

Serves 4

- **3** TABLESPOONS SOY SAUCE
- **6** GREEN ONIONS, THINLY SLICED
- **4** CLOVES GARLIC, COARSELY CHOPPED
- **1** TABLESPOON CHOPPED FRESH GINGER
- **1½** TEASPOONS CHILI POWDER
- **1** TEASPOON GROUND CORIANDER
- **½** TEASPOON PEPPER
- **4** SKINLESS, BONELESS CHICKEN BREAST HALVES (ABOUT 1¼ POUNDS)
- **3** LARGE RED PEPPERS, HALVED, CHARRED AND PEELED
- **¼** CUP RICE WINE OR CIDER VINEGAR
- **½** TEASPOON RED PEPPER FLAKES
- **½** TEASPOON SALT
- **2** TABLESPOONS PLUS 1 TEASPOON SUGAR

1 In food processor or blender, combine soy sauce, green onions, 3 cloves garlic, ginger, chili powder, coriander and pepper; process until smooth. Place soy mixture in sturdy plastic bag or shallow bowl. Add chicken; cover or seal tightly and refrigerate 30 minutes or up to 12 hours.

2 Prepare broiler or grill according to manufacturer's directions. Broil or grill chicken 4 inches from heat source until lightly browned, about 4 minutes. Turn; broil or grill until chicken is thoroughly cooked, about 4 to 6 minutes.

3 In food processor or blender, place 4 red pepper halves; process until smooth. Cut remaining 2 red pepper halves into thin strips.

4 In small saucepan, combine remaining clove garlic, pepper purée, vinegar, red pepper flakes and salt over medium heat. Bring to a boil. Stir in sugar; cook until sugar is dissolved and sauce is syrupy, about 4 minutes.

5 Stir in reserved red pepper strips. Serve chicken topped with red pepper sauce.

PREPARATION TIP

Follow Steps 3 and 4 to make just the red chili sauce and use as a topping for hamburgers, steak, sliced cooked chicken and even turkey.

Calories: 246 · Protein: 35 g
Fat: 5 g/19% calories from fat · Carbohydrate: 14 g
Cholesterol: 89 mg · Sodium: 1,124 mg

Devilish Drumsticks with Cheese Sauce

A takeoff on Buffalo Wings, which were first created in a Buffalo, New York, restaurant, these spicy drumsticks offer more meat per serving and ease of preparation.

Serves 4

- **1** PACKAGE (3 OUNCES) CREAM CHEESE, AT ROOM TEMPERATURE
- **¼** CUP PLAIN YOGURT
- **2** TABLESPOONS CHOPPED PARSLEY (OPTIONAL)
- **1** CLOVE GARLIC, MINCED
- **½** TEASPOON DRIED OREGANO
- **¼** TEASPOON SALT
- **¼** TEASPOON PEPPER
- **3** TABLESPOONS BUTTER OR MARGARINE, MELTED
- **3** TABLESPOONS HOT PEPPER SAUCE
- **8** CHICKEN DRUMSTICKS (ABOUT 1¾ POUNDS)

1 Preheat broiler. Line broiler pan with foil and set aside.

2 In small bowl, beat cream cheese, yogurt, parsley, if desired, garlic, oregano, salt and pepper until well mixed. Cover and refrigerate until serving time.

3 In shallow bowl, combine butter and hot pepper sauce. Dip each drumstick into butter mixture to completely coat; place on prepared pan. Broil 4 inches from heat source until skin is golden, about 7 minutes. Turn; cook until skin is golden, about 7 to 10 minutes.

4 Serve cooked drumsticks with cream cheese-yogurt sauce.

PREPARATION TIP

Everything can be made ahead and served cold or at room temperature. The sauce can be made up to 3 days in advance.

Calories: 339 · Protein: 26 g
Fat: 25 g/66% calories from fat · Carbohydrate: 2 g
Cholesterol: 123 mg · Sodium: 605 mg

METRIC CONVERSIONS

DRY INGREDIENTS

Baking powder/soda	1 tsp. = 3 grams
Cornmeal	1 cup = 150 grams
Cornstarch	¼ cup = 30 grams
FLOUR	
All-purpose, unsifted	1 cup = 120 grams
Cake or pastry, sifted	1 cup = 100 grams
Whole-wheat, unsifted	1 cup = 125 grams
Nuts, coarsely chopped	1 cup = 140 grams
Herbs, dry	1 tsp. = 2 grams
Rice, uncooked	1 cup = 150 grams
Salt	1 tsp. = 5 grams
Spices, ground	1 tsp. = 2 grams
SUGAR	
Granulated	1 tsp. = 5 grams
	1 tbsp. = 15 grams
	1 cup = 200 grams
Confectioners'	1 cup = 110 grams
Brown, packed	1 cup = 220 grams

FATS, OILS, AND CHEESE

Butter	8 tablespoons = ½ cup = 4 ounces = 125 grams
Shortening or lard	1 cup = 250 grams
Vegetable oil	¼ cup = 60 ml
Cheese, grated	1 cup = 4 ounces = 120 grams

LIQUID MEASURES

1 tablespoon = 15 ml
1 fluid ounce = 30 ml
¼ cup = 60 ml
⅓ cup = 80 ml
½ cup = 125 ml
¾ cup = 185 ml
1 cup = 250 ml
1 quart = 1 liter

WEIGHTS

1 ounce = 30 grams
1 pound = 450 grams
2.2 pounds = 1 kilogram

FAHRENHEIT/CELSIUS CONVERSIONS

$9/5C + 32 = F$
$(F-32)5/9 = C$

OVEN TEMPERATURES

°Fahrenheit	°Celsius
250 (low oven)	120
300	150
325	160
350 (moderate oven)	175
400	200
450	230
500 (very hot oven)	260

INDEX